Scoot Over, Skinny

Scoot Over, Skinny

The FAT Nonfiction Anthology

EDITED BY

Donna Jarrell and Ira Sukrungruang

A Harvest Original • Harcourt, Inc.

Orlando   Austin   New York   San Diego   Toronto   London www.HarcourtBooks.com

Library of Congress Cataloging-in-Publication Data
Scoot over, skinny: the fat nonfiction anthology / edited by Donna Jarrell and
Ira Sukrungruang.
p. cm.
"A harvest original."
ISBN 0-15-603022-5
1. Overweight persons. 2. Obesity. I. Jarrell, Donna. II. Sukrungruang, Ira.
RC628.S385 2004
616.3'98—dc22   2004014920

Text set in Garamond MT
Designed by Cathy Riggs

Printed in the United States of America
First edition
A C E G I K J H F D B

Permissions Acknowledgments begin on page 293 and constitute a continuation
of the copyright page.

Contents

Acknowledgments

Much appreciation to our editor, Ann Patty, whose vision for this anthology substantially enriched its contents. And thanks to many others at Harcourt, particularly Evan Boorstyn and Sloane Miller. An affectionate swat on the tush for K. C. Wolfe, who logged tons of hours at the copier and on the phone doing a lot of the grunt work. A cheeky Manhattan air kiss for Bob Mecoy, a fantastic coach and agent. And a big fat hug to all the writers whose essays allow this book to fulfill its ambition. No acknowledgment would be complete without recognizing our friends and families, the backbone of our accomplishments.

Finally, Ira thanks Donna. Donna thanks Ira. Here's to a fun, productive partnership. May our big fat friendship sustain us for many years to come.

Fat as a Matter of Fact

Donna is fat. Ira is fat. As a matter of fact, over half of the American population is fat. And not for a moment are we allowed to forget it.

On the drive home from work, a billboard that not so very long ago seduced consumers with the Marlboro man now advertises the gastric bypass surgery unit of a nearby hospital: "If you're one hundred or more pounds overweight," whispered the billboard, "your insurance may cover the costs of surgery." The corner market, whose windows were once stuffed with our favorite junk foods, has now been replaced by the neighborhood sports and fitness center, whose door endlessly swings with the motion of hard, lean, in-your-face bodies: "See what a little discipline and willpower can do." Protein bars, diet drinks, and fat-free, low/no-carb foods, which have earned a place alongside bread, milk, and other staples in the main aisles of the grocery store, shout from shelves: "You? Control *your* appetite?" Even the well-meaning consolation of a lover—*What really counts is on the inside*—or the encouragement of a friend—*Just do it!*—stings with the suggestion of our unwieldy size.

No longer are we, the Fat, simply the nail under the bully's hammer. In this new millennium, the long skinny finger of American culture is pointedly aimed at us. The government has declared a war on fat. Medicare has pathologized fat. The U.S. Congress is entertaining a "fat tax" and has proposed a "National Obesity Awareness Month." In the past year, several organizations have convened for obesity summits: fat has been decried a "national emergency."

For the government and the health-care agencies, for the taxpayer and the media, for the scientist and for the skinny, the obesity crisis is political. It's clinical, economical, theoretical, even sensational. But the obesity crisis *inside* a fat life is personal. In here, our bellies protrude, our chins drape, our legs rub together; our skin chafes and sweat puddles between the folds of our blubber. Yes, our bodies are fat, but so are our inner selves.

Fat is the adjective that leaps in front of every other descriptor: fat writer, fat professor, fat mother, fat friend. Fat insulates our bodies and fat infiltrates our identities. We cannot limit our loathing to our distorted size and shape: We hate ourselves. We cannot see our bodies as simply fat: We see our characters as seriously flawed. Each day we bring our flesh into a public that prizes leanness, each day we carry our heavy and cumbersome bodies through a world that idolizes speed and efficiency, we suffer shame. Until recently, that shame has kept us silent.

By bringing these essays together, we hope to expand the dialogue on obesity, to bring to the discussion an inside view. We are speaking out, speaking up, speaking back: Scoot over, skinny, the Fat have a few things of their own to say about obesity, and frankly, we want to discuss more than the mechanics of how to lose weight or where to place the blame. Instead of containing fat within the clinical paradigm, we want to turn fat loose, to spill the discussion onto the landscape of our humanity, to converse on the topic within the context of love and loss and need and desire, within the context of relationships with ourselves and others. Fat is more than a social issue, it's more than a number on a scale: fat is an experience.

Each essay in this book says something important about fat, something original and insightful, something familiar or frightening or shocking. These essays explore fat-identity; they strip the surface off fat, debunk fat myths and stereotypes, and educate readers about the physical and emotional complexities of the fat experience. They examine the prejudice faced by the fat—sometimes self-directed—and the paradoxes inherent in the fat experience.

Though fat is more than a physical issue, contemplating fat provokes Michael Martone to reflect on the astonishing abilities of the human body to expand and contract as he writes about his wife's pregnancies and his own sympathetic weight gain. In "Tight Fits," Ira Sukrungruang cannot ignore his physicality as he flies to Thailand, the home of his slimmer ancestors. Steven A. Shaw asserts "Fat Guys Kick Ass," and wonders why we ignore the fat body at all—fat is powerful, and fat men should be proud. However, for the morbidly obese, the fat body becomes more than an obstacle; it becomes a burden. In "The Man Who Couldn't Stop Eating," Atul Gawande tells the story of a man who undergoes Roux-en-Y gastric bypass because he is so obese he can barely walk, so obese that the normal demands of everyday life screech to a halt.

The physical experience of fat is inextricable from the emotional experience. For a dieter, the mental struggle is often more exhausting than physical exertion. We lose fat. We gain it back. We lose. We gain. One moment the fat body doesn't seem intrusive; we barely notice our size. The next moment fat weighs us down in every way. Pam Houston's essay "Out of Habit, I Start Apologizing," struggles with this dichotomy. At one point she feels strong and powerful, navigating a raft through rough river water, but then finds herself comparing her large body (unfavorably, of course) to petite ones.

For many of these authors body-size comparison weighs heavily on the mind and breeds unrealistic ideas.

Ridding oneself of fat becomes an obsession, a religion: calories a list of sins, dieting a structure for life. If you follow the creed to the letter, you get into heaven: you're rewarded with a thin body. But can a religion with the body as both deity and devil be satisfying? In "Letting Myself Go," Sallie Tisdale doesn't think so. She writes of her dire dieting days and how the cultural demands placed on women's bodies almost strangled her. These demands feed a fear of fat. For years, this same fear pushed Anne Lamott away from food. Her essay "Hunger" recounts her struggles with food, and how, at thirty-three, her body and her psyche finally began to communicate. In "Queen of the Gym," Cheryl Peck wonders how a fat woman can overcome skinny intimidation and get fit in a gym filled with workout princes and princesses.

Neither does the fat experience exist in a vacuum. Though it is the individual who experiences fat, the culture in which we live profoundly affects that experience. Sarah Fenske details the shocking side of fat prejudice in "Big Game Hunters," where she discusses with thin men the degrading act of "hogging"—pursuing and persecuting fat women for sex. Culturally sanctioned prejudice is one of the things Sondra Solovay, a lawyer and fat activist, addresses in "Now You See Me, Now You Don't," in which she laments the social forces that pushed one woman into unnecessary and fatal weight-loss surgery. David Sedaris presents a bitingly funny essay that explores a family's fat prejudice in "A Shiner Like a Diamond," when he recounts how his sister donned a fat suit for a visit home to their fat-fearing father. And in perhaps the bravest pieces in the book, Irving Yalom and Lori Gottlieb confront their own biases against fat in "The Fat Lady" and "Fat Like Him."

Fat is not simple. In fact, fat is full of contradictions and paradoxes. In "On Being Invisible," Natalie Kusz argues that even though an over-large presence occupies more physical space, fat individuals are invisible. Fat becomes an identifying characteristic that makes everything else about us irrelevant. In the essay "Fatland," Stephen Kuusisto consciously chooses to become fat to deter school-yard bullies from his blindness, an example of how fat's bulk can hide other marks of difference. In "Big Time," Victor LaValle doesn't hide anything. He discusses his sexuality as a fat man and the peculiar combination of vanity and business acumen that drove him to lose weight. And finally, using the same unyielding honesty as LaValle, Donna Jarrell writes about the search for body acceptance and fat forgiveness in the very place where she is most exposed, as a "Fat Lady Nuding."

We hope that you, our readers, appreciate the depth and breadth of the writing in this book; that you are as delighted and angered, as touched and surprised as we were. But most of all, we hope that this conversation about fat is recognized for what it really is: a conversation about the human condition, in all its pathos and glory.

—DONNA JARRELL AND IRA SUKRUNGRUANG

Scoot Over, Skinny

Letting Myself Go

I don't know how much I weigh these days, though I can make a good guess. For years I'd known that number, sometimes within a quarter pound, known how it changed from day to day and hour to hour. I want to weigh myself now; I lean toward the scale in the next room, imagine standing there, lining up the balance. But I don't do it. Going this long, starting to break the scale's spell—it's like waking up suddenly sober.

By the time I was sixteen years old I had reached my adult height of five feet six inches and weighed 164 pounds. I weighed 164 pounds before and after a healthy pregnancy. I assume I weigh about the same now; nothing significant seems to have happened to my body, this same old body I've had all these years. I usually wear a size 14, a common clothing size for American women. On bad days

I think my body looks lumpy and misshapen. On my good days, which are more frequent lately, I think I look plush and strong; I think I look like a lot of women whose bodies and lives I admire.

I'm not sure when the word "fat" first sounded pejorative to me, or when I first applied it to myself. My grandmother was a petite woman, the only one in my family. She stole food from other people's plates, and hid the debris of her own meals so that no one would know how much she ate. My mother was a size 14, like me, all her adult life; we shared clothes. She fretted endlessly over food scales, calorie counters, and diet books. She didn't want to quit smoking because she was afraid she would gain weight, and she worried about her weight until she died of cancer. Dieting was always in my mother's way, always there in the conversations above my head, the dialogue of stocky women. But I was strong and healthy and didn't pay too much attention to my weight until I was grown.

It probably wouldn't have been possible for me to escape forever. It doesn't matter that whole human epochs have celebrated big men and women, because the brief period in which I live does not; since I was born, even the voluptuous calendar girl has gone. Today's models, the women whose pictures I see constantly, unavoidably, grow more minimal by the day. When I berate myself for not looking like whomever I think I should look like that day, I don't really care that no one looks like that. I don't care that Michelle Pfeiffer doesn't look like the photographs I see of

Michelle Pfeiffer. I want to look—think I should look—
like the photographs. I want her little miracles: the makeup
artists, photographers, and computer imagers who can add
a mole, remove a scar, lift the breasts, widen the eyes, narrow the hips, flatten the curves. The final product is what I
see, have seen my whole adult life. And I've seen this: Even
when big people become celebrities, their weight is constantly remarked upon and scrutinized; their successes
seem always to be *in spite of* their weight. I thought my successes must be too.

I feel myself expand and diminish from day to day,
sometimes from hour to hour. If I tell someone my weight,
I change in their eyes: I become bigger or smaller, better or
worse, depending on what that number, my weight, means
to them. I know many men and women, young and old,
gay and straight, who look fine, whom I love to see and
whose faces and forms I cherish, who despise themselves
for their weight. For their ordinary, human bodies. We are
simply bigger than we think we should be. We always talk
about weight in terms of gains and losses, and don't wonder at the strangeness of the words. In trying always to lose
weight, we've lost hope of simply being seen for ourselves.

My weight has never actually affected anything—it's
never seemed to mean anything one way or the other to
how I lived. Yet for many years I've felt quite bad about
it. After a time, the number on the scale became my to-
tem, more important than my experience—it was layered,
metaphorical, *metaphysical*, and it had bewitching power. I

thought if I could change that number I could change my life.

In my mid-twenties I started secretly taking diet pills. They made me feel strange, half crazed, vaguely nauseated. I lost about twenty-five pounds, dropped two sizes, and bought new clothes. I developed rituals and taboos around food, ate very little, and continued to lose weight. For a long time afterward I thought it only coincidental that with every passing week I also grew more depressed and irritable.

I could recite the details, but they're remarkable only for being so common. I lost more weight until I was rather thin, and then I gained it all back. It came back slowly, pound by pound, in spite of erratic and melancholy and sometimes frantic dieting, dieting I clung to even though being thin had changed nothing, had meant nothing to my life except that I was thin. Looking back, I remember blinding moments of shame and lightning-bright moments of clearheadedness, which inevitably gave way to rage at the time I'd wasted—rage that eventually would become, once again, self-disgust and the urge to lose weight. So it went, until I weighed exactly what I'd weighed when I began.

I used to be attracted to the sharp angles of the chronic dieter—the caffeine-wild, chain-smoking, skinny women I see sometimes. I considered them a pinnacle not of beauty but of will. Even after I gained back my weight, I wanted to be like that, controlled and persevering, live that underfed life so unlike my own rather sensual and disorderly existence. I felt I should always be dieting, for the dieting of it; dieting had become a rule, a given, a constant. Every ordinary value is distorted in this lens. I felt guilty for not being completely absorbed in my diet, for getting distracted, for not caring enough all the time. The fat person's character flaw is a lack of narcissism. She's let herself go.

So I would begin again—and at first it would all seem so...easy. Simple arithmetic. After all, 3,500 calories equal one pound of fat—so the books and articles by the thousands say. I would calculate how long it would take to achieve the magic number on the scale, to succeed, to win. All past failures were suppressed. If 3,500 calories equal one pound, all I needed to do was cut 3,500 calories out of my intake every week. The first few days of a new diet would be colored with a sense of control—organization and planning, power over the self. Then the basic futile misery took over.

I would weigh myself with foreboding, and my weight would determine how went the rest of my day, my week, my life. When 3,500 calories didn't equal one pound lost after all, I figured it was my body that was flawed, not the theory. One friend, who had tried for years to lose weight following prescribed diets, made what she called "an amazing discovery." The real secret to a diet, she said, was that you had to be willing to be hungry *all the time*. You had to eat even less than the diet allowed.

I believed that being thin would make me happy. Such a pernicious, enduring belief. I lost weight and wasn't happy and saw that elusive happiness disappear in a vanishing point, requiring more—more self-disgust, more of the misery of dieting. Knowing all that I know now about the biology and anthropology of weight, knowing that people naturally come in many shapes and sizes, knowing that diets are bad for me and won't make me thin—sometimes none of this matters. I look in the mirror and think: Who am I kidding? *I've got to do something about myself.* Only then will this vague discontent disappear. Then I'll be loved.

For ages humans believed that the body helped create the personality, from the humors of Galen to W. H. Sheldon's somatotypes. Sheldon distinguished among three templates—endomorph, mesomorph, and ectomorph— and combined them into hundreds of variations with physical, emotional, and psychological characteristics. When I read about weight now, I see the potent shift in the last few decades: The modern culture of dieting is based on the idea that the personality creates the body. Our size must be in some way voluntary, or else it wouldn't be subject to change. A lot of my misery over my weight wasn't about how I looked at all. I was miserable because I believed *I*

was bad, not my body. I felt truly reduced then, reduced to being just a body and nothing more.

Fat is perceived as an *act* rather than a thing. It is anti-social, and curable through the application of social controls. Even the feminist revisions of dieting, so powerful in themselves, pick up the theme: the hungry, empty heart; the woman seeking release from sexual assault, or the man from the loss of the mother, through food and fat. Fat is now a symbol not of the personality but of the soul—the cluttered, neurotic, immature soul.

Fat people eat for "mere gratification," I read, as though no one else does. Their weight is *intentioned*, they simply eat "too much," their flesh is lazy flesh. Whenever I went on a diet, eating became cheating. One pretzel was cheating. Two apples instead of one was cheating—a large potato instead of a small, carrots instead of broccoli. It didn't matter which diet I was on; diets have failure built in, failure is in the definition. Every substitution—even carrots for broccoli—was a triumph of desire over will. When I dieted, I didn't feel pious just for sticking to the rules. I felt condemned for the act of eating itself, as though my hunger were never normal. My penance was to not eat at all.

My attitude toward food became quite corrupt. I came, in fact, to subconsciously believe food itself was corrupt. Diet books often distinguish between "real" and "unreal" hunger, so that *correct* eating is hollowed out, unemotional. A friend of mine who thinks of herself as a compulsive eater says she feels bad only when she eats for pleasure: "Why?" I ask, and she says, "Because I'm eating food I don't need." A few years ago I might have admired that. Now I try to imagine a world where we eat only food we need, and it seems inhuman. I imagine a world devoid of holidays and wedding feasts, wakes and reunions, a unique shared joy. "What's wrong with eating a cookie because you like cookies?" I ask her, and she hasn't got an answer. These aren't rational beliefs, any more than the unnecessary pleasure of ice cream is rational. Dieting presumes pleasure to be an insignificant, or at least malleable, human motive.

I felt no joy in being thin—it was just work, something I had to do. But when I began to gain back the weight, I felt despair. I started reading about the "recidivism" of dieting. I wondered if I had myself to blame not only for needing to diet in the first place but for dieting itself, the weight inevitably regained. I joined organized weight-loss programs, spent a lot of money, listened to lectures I didn't believe on quack nutrition, ate awful, processed diet foods. I sat in groups and applauded people who'd lost a half pound, feeling smug because I'd lost a pound and a half. I felt ill much of the time, found exercise increasingly difficult, cried often. And I thought that if I could only lose a little weight, everything would be all right.

When I say to someone "I'm fat," I hear, "Oh, no! You're not *fat*! You're just—" What? Plump? Big-boned? Rubenesque? I'm just *not thin*. That's crime enough. I began this story by stating my weight. I said it all at once, trying to forget it and take away its power; I said it to be done being scared. Doing so, saying it out loud like that, felt like confessing a mortal sin. I have to bite my tongue not to seek reassurance, not to defend myself, not to plead. I see an old friend for the first time in years, and she comments on how much my son looks like me—"except, of course, he's not chubby." "Look who's talking," I reply, through clenched teeth. This pettiness is never far away; concern with my weight evokes the smallest, meanest parts of me. I look at another woman passing on the street and think, At least I'm not *that* fat.

Recently I was talking with a friend who is naturally slender about a mutual acquaintance who is quite large. To my surprise my friend reproached this woman because she had seen her eating a cookie at lunchtime. "How is she going to lose weight that way?" my friend wondered. When you are as fat as our acquaintance is, you are primarily, fundamentally, seen as fat. It is your essential characteristic. There are so many presumptions in my friend's casual, cruel remark. She assumes that this woman should diet all the time—and that she *can*. She pronounces whole categories of food to be denied her. She sees her unwillingness to behave in this externally prescribed way, even for a moment, as an act of rebellion. In his story "A Hunger Artist," Kafka writes that the guards of the fasting man were "usually butchers, strangely enough." Not so strange, I think.

I know that the world, even if it views me as over-weight (and I'm not sure it really does), clearly makes a distinction between me and this very big woman. I would rather stand with her and not against her, see her for all she is besides fat. But I know our experiences aren't the same. My thin friend assumes my fat friend is unhappy because she is fat: Therefore, if she loses weight she will be happy. My fat friend has a happy marriage and family and a good career, but insofar as her weight is a source of misery, I think she would be much happier if she could eat her cookie in peace, if people would shut up and leave her weight alone. But the world never lets up when you are her size; she cannot walk to the bank without risking insult. Her fat is seen as perverse bad manners. I have no doubt she would be rid of the fat if she could be. If my left-handedness invited the criticism her weight does, I would want to cut that hand off.

In these last several years I seem to have had an infinite number of conversations about dieting. They are really all the same conversation—weight is lost, then weight is gained back. This repetition finally began to sink in. Why did everyone sooner or later have the same experience? (My friend who had learned to be hungry all the time gained back all the weight she had lost and more, just like the rest of us.) Was it really our bodies that were flawed? I began reading the biology of weight more carefully, reading the fine print in the endless studies. There is, in fact, a preponderance of evidence disputing our commonly held assumptions about weight.

The predominant biological myth of weight is that thin people live longer than fat people. The truth is far more complicated. (Some deaths of fat people attributed to heart disease seem actually to have been the result of radical dieting.) If health were our real concern, it would be dieting we questioned, not weight. The current ideal of thinness has never been held before, except as a religious ideal; the underfed body is the martyr's body. Even if people can lose weight, maintaining an artificially low weight for any period of time requires a kind of starvation. Lots of people are naturally thin, but for those who are not, dieting is an unnatural act; biology rebels. The metabolism of the hungry body can change inalterably, making it ever harder and harder to stay thin. I think chronic dieting made me gain weight—not only pounds, but fat. This equation seemed so strange at first that I couldn't believe it. But the weight I put back on after losing was much more stubborn than the original weight. I had lost it by taking diet pills and not eating much of anything at all for quite a long time. I haven't touched the pills again, but not eating much of anything no longer works.

When Oprah Winfrey first revealed her lost weight, I didn't envy her. I thought, She's in trouble now. I knew, I was certain, she would gain it back; I believed she was biologically destined to do so. The tabloid headlines blamed it

on a cheeseburger or mashed potatoes; they screamed
OPRAH PASSES 200 POUNDS, and I cringed at her misery and
how the world wouldn't let up, wouldn't leave her alone,
wouldn't let her be anything else. How dare the world do
this to anyone? I thought, and then realized I did it to
myself.

The "Ideal Weight" charts my mother used were at
their lowest acceptable-weight ranges in the 1950s, when I
was a child. They were based on sketchy and often inaccu-
rate actuarial evidence, using, for the most part, data on
northern Europeans and allowing for the most minimal
differences in size for a population of less than half a bil-
lion people. I never fit those weight charts, I was always
just outside the pale. As an adult, when I would join an
organized diet program, I accepted their version of my
Weight Goal as gospel, knowing it would be virtually impossible to reach. But reach I tried; that's what one does
with gospel. Only in the last few years have the weight
tables begun to climb back into the world of the average
human. The newest ones distinguish by gender, frame, and
age. And suddenly I'm not off the charts anymore. I have a
place.

A man who is attracted to fat women says, "I actually
have less specific physical criteria than most men. I'm attracted to women who weigh 170 or 270 or 370. Most men
are only attracted to women who weigh between 100 and
135. So who's got more of a fetish?" We look at fat as a
problem of the fat person. Rarely do the tables get turned,

rarely do we imagine that it might be the viewer, not the viewed, who is limited. What the hell is wrong with *them*, anyway? Do they believe everything they see on television?

My friend Phil, who is chronically and almost painfully thin, admitted that in his search for a partner he finds himself prejudiced against fat women. He seemed genuinely bewildered by this. I didn't jump to reassure him that such prejudice is hard to resist. What I did was bite my tongue at my urge to be reassured by him, to be told that I, at least, wasn't fat. That over the centuries humans have been inclined to prefer extra flesh rather than the other way around seems unimportant. All we see now tells us otherwise. Why does my kindhearted friend criticize another woman for eating a cookie when she would never dream of commenting in such a way on another person's race or sexual orientation or disability? Deprivation is the dystopian ideal.

My mother called her endless diets "reducing plans." Reduction, the diminution of women, is the opposite of feminism, as Kim Chernin points out in *The Obsession*. Smallness is what feminism strives against, the smallness that women confront everywhere. All of women's spaces are smaller than those of men, often inadequate, without privacy. Furniture designers distinguish between a man's and a woman's chair, because women don't spread out like men. (A sprawling woman means only one thing.) Even our voices are kept down. By embracing dieting I was rejecting a lot I held dear, and the emotional dissonance that created just seemed like one more necessary evil.

A fashion magazine recently celebrated the return of the "well-fed" body; a particular model was said to be "the archetype of the new womanly woman...stately, powerful." She is a size 8. The images of women presented to us, images claiming so maliciously to be the images of women's whole lives, are not merely social fictions. They are *absolute* fictions; they can't exist. How would it feel, I began to wonder, to cultivate my own real womanliness rather than despise it? Because it was my fleshy curves I wanted to be rid of, after all. I dreamed of having a boy's body, smooth, hipless, lean. A body rapt with possibility, a receptive body suspended before the storms of maturity. A dear friend of mine, nursing her second child, weeps at her newly voluptuous body. She loves her children and hates her own motherliness, wanting to be unripened again, to be a bud and not a flower.

Recently I've started shopping occasionally at stores for "large women," where the smallest size is a 14. In department stores the size 12 and 14 and 16 clothes are kept in a ghetto called the Women's Department. (And who would want that, to be the size of a woman? We all dream of being "juniors" instead.) In the specialty stores the clerks are usually big women and the customers are big too, big like a lot of women in my life—friends, my sister, my mother and aunts. Not long ago I bought a pair of jeans at Lane Bryant and then walked through the mall to the Gap, with its shelves of generic clothing. I flicked through the clearance rack and suddenly remembered the Lane Bryant shopping bag in my hand and its enormous weight, the sheer heaviness of that brand name shouting to the world. The shout is that I've let myself go. I still feel like crying out sometimes: Can't I feel *satisfied*? But I am not supposed to be satisfied, not allowed to be satisfied. My discontent fuels the market; I need to be afraid in order to fully participate.

American culture, which has produced our dieting mania, does more than reward privation and acquisition at the same time: It actually associates them with each other. Read the ads: The virtuous runner's reward is a new pair of $180 running shoes. The fat person is thought to be impulsive, indulgent, but insufficiently or incorrectly greedy, greedy for the wrong thing. The fat person lacks ambition. The young executive is complimented for being "hungry"; he is "starved for success." We are teased with what we will *have* if we are willing to *have not* for a time. A dieting friend, avoiding the food on my table, says, "I'm just dying for a bite of that."

Dieters are the perfect consumers: They never get enough. The dieter wistfully imagines food without substance, food that is not food, that begs the definition of food, because food is the problem. Even the ways we *don't eat* are based in class. The middle class don't eat in support groups. The poor can't afford not to eat at all. The rich hire someone to not eat with them in private. Hordes of

Americans now relish the right to eat at the very top of the food chain all the time, predators living only on meat and calling it deprivation. Dieting is an emblem of capitalism. It has a venal heart.

The possibility of living another way, living without dieting, began to take root in my mind a few years ago, and finally my second trip through Weight Watchers ended dieting for me. This last time I just couldn't stand the details, the same kind of details I'd seen and despised in other programs, on other diets: the scent of resignation, the weighing-in by the quarter pound, the before-and-after photographs of group leaders prominently displayed. Jean Nidetch, the founder of Weight Watchers, says, "Most fat people need to be hurt badly before they do something about themselves." She mocks every aspect of our need for food, of a person's sense of entitlement to food, of daring to *eat what we want.* Weight Watchers refuses to release its own weight charts except to say they make no distinction for frame size; neither has the organization ever released statistics on how many people who lose weight on the program eventually gain it back. I hated the endlessness of it, the turning of food into portions and exchanges, everything measured out, permitted, denied. I hated the very idea of "maintenance." Finally I realized I didn't just hate the diet. I was sick of the way I acted on a diet, the way I whined, my niggardly, penny-pinching behavior. What I liked in myself seemed to shrivel and disappear when I dieted. Slowly, slowly I saw these things. I saw that my pain was cut from whole cloth, imaginary, my own invention. I saw how much time I'd spent on something ephemeral, something that simply wasn't important, didn't matter. I saw that the real point of dieting is dieting—to not be done with it, ever.

I looked in the mirror and saw a woman, with flesh, curves, muscles, a few stretch marks, the beginnings of wrinkles, with strength and softness in equal measure. My body is the one part of me that is always, undeniably, here. To like myself means to be, literally, shameless, to be wanton in the pleasures of being inside a body. I feel *loose* this way, a little abandoned, a little dangerous. That first feeling of liking my body—not being resigned to it or despairing of change, but actually *liking* it—was tentative and guilty and frightening. It was alarming, because it was the way I'd felt as a child, before the world had interfered. Because surely I was wrong; I knew, I'd known for so long, that my body wasn't all right this way. I was afraid even to act as though I were all right: I was afraid that by doing so I'd be acting a fool.

For a time I was thin. I remember—and what I remember is nothing special—strain, a kind of hollowness, the same troubles and fears, and no magic. So I imagine losing weight again. If the world applauded, would this comfort me? Or would it only compromise whatever approval the world gives me now? What else will be required of me besides thinness? What will happen to me if I get sick, or lose the use of a limb, or, God forbid, grow old?

By fussing endlessly over my body, I've ceased to inhabit it. I'm trying to reverse this equation now, to trust my body and enter it again with a whole heart. I know more now than I used to about what constitutes "happy" and "unhappy," what the depths and textures of contentment are like. By letting go of dieting, I free up mental and emotional room. I have more space, I can move. The pursuit of another, elusive body, the body someone else says I should have, is a terrible distraction, a sidetracking that might have lasted my whole life long. By letting myself go, I go places.

Each of us in this culture, this twisted, inchoate culture, has to choose between battles: One battle is against the cultural ideal, and the other is against ourselves. I've chosen to stop fighting myself. Maybe I'm tilting at windmills; the cultural ideal is ever-changing, out of my control. It's not a cerebral journey, except insofar as I have to remind myself to stop counting, to stop thinking in terms of numbers. I know, even now that I've quit dieting and eat what I want, how many calories I take in every day. If I eat as I please, I eat a lot one day and very little the next; I skip meals and snack at odd times. My nourishment is good— as far as nutrition is concerned, I'm in much better shape than when I was dieting. I know that the small losses and gains in my weight over a period of time aren't simply related to the number of calories I eat. Someone asked me not long ago how I could possibly know my calorie intake if I'm not dieting (the implication being, perhaps, that I'm dieting secretly). I know because calorie counts and grams of fat and fiber are embedded in me. I have to work to *not* think of them, and I have to learn to not think of them in order to really live without fear.

When I look, *really* look, at the people I see every day on the street, I see a jungle of bodies, a community of women and men growing every which way like lush plants, growing tall and short and slender and round, hairy and hairless, dark and pale and soft and hard and glorious. Do I look around at the multitudes and think all these people— all these people who are like me and not like me, who are various and different—are not loved or lovable? Lately, everyone's body interests me, every body is desirable in some way. I see how muscles and skin shift with move- ment; I sense a cornucopia of flesh in the world. In the midst of it I am a little capacious and unruly.

I repeat with Walt Whitman, "I dote on myself...there is that lot of me, and all so luscious." I'm eating better, ex- ercising more, feeling fine—and then I catch myself think- ing *Maybe I'll lose some weight.* But my mood changes or my attention is caught by something else, something deeper, more lingering. Then I can catch a glimpse of myself by accident and think only: That's me. My face, my hips, my hands. Myself.

On Being Invisible

I am a big—a very big—woman. I mention this up front because a logical person might expect wide visibility to accompany my wide body, the way, say, a four-inch-tall newspaper headline (SENATOR DITCHES WIFE FOR CHEERLEADER) catches the eye more easily than a tiny ad in the classifieds (dwm seeks fling with bimbo). People of all occupations understand (regardless of what we tell men) that size *does* make a difference, especially perceptibility-wise: a publicist prefers a billboard to a poster; an aging bookworm supports her library habit by moving on to large-print books; a pope exalts God by painting the whole church ceiling, not just a wee corner by the door. To make a thing seen, we magnify it, blow it up, set the photocopier to "Enlarge."

Except—I can attest to this—when it comes to people of size. Not only are we not *more* visible because of our bigness, we are in fact *in*visible because of it. Begin with a minor example: A great many people cannot distinguish me from my sister (both of us fat), although I wear an eye patch and she does not, she wears glasses and I do not, and her shyness and unassuming dark wardrobe differ significantly from my own brassy attitude, loud color scheme, and pierced nose. A woman in our hometown, whose son was in school with my sister, and who had both of us to her house numerous times during childhood, asks me to lunch every time I am home. Over pizza and espresso, we get to reminiscing, and she says, "I've wondered if you still play the flute" (that was my sister), "It was so funny when you beat my son at the spelling bee" (that was me), "You were always so good at math" (my sister), and so on. From our first lunch date I have realized (but have never known what to do about it) that not only does this woman—who knew us both, growing up, and who does not to my knowledge suffer from Alzheimer's—fail to distinguish between my sister and me, *she thinks there is only one of us.*

Okay, you might say. But people mix up family members all the time. We've all done it. It proves not a thing about invisibility.

How, then, would you explain my friend's recent experience at the shoe store? On her lunch break one day, Maxine was sitting next to a stranger at Footwear For

Females, both of them waiting for the same service person to bring out the shoes they'd requested. One of the women was dark-haired and Hispanic, the other blond and white; one wore a black worsted business suit, the other a poppy-red dress revealing serious *décolletage;* one wanted to try on flat black penny loafers, the other a pair of sequined red pumps with three-inch heels. The salesperson returned with both pairs of shoes, handing them out to the wrong customers: glittery pumps to the business suit and loafers to the red dress. Clearly, he had made no distinction between these women of differing races, fashion statements, and sexual personae. What had made them invisible to him? Maxine believed, and I can think of no other explanation, that it was the single thing she had in common with the stranger: They were both fat.

The fact is, the old racist attitude that "all black (or Asian or Latin) people look alike" also applies to fat people, with the same main corollary: We look alike to other beings because they cannot see us at all. In the last ten years I have accumulated maybe 80,000 frequent-flyer miles, and almost never have I worn a seat belt, or been reprimanded by a flight attendant. When the attendants make their final check up and down the aisles (I've noticed them making four passes now instead of two, probably because of the rise in plane crashes), they invariably skip my aisle entirely—in part, I'm sure, because they are afraid to look at me too closely (a lot of thin people believe cellulite to be an airborne contagion). To test my invisibility theory, though, I've experimented with making my seatbeltlessness impossible to miss; I've stretched the left half of the belt forward and tucked it into the magazine pouch, and I've even sat swinging it, like a flapper's beads, from my hand. The attendants approach, speak to the kid in front of me ("tray table up, please"), and pass me right by. I swear it, I know it, they think my seat is empty.

Which severely tempts me, I tell you, to turn to crime. I could walk into any bank, rifle all the cash drawers, *ask the tellers for change,* and walk out without anyone remembering later I had been there. All that cloak-of-invisibility crap over which comic book villains struggle could be solved with one solid piece of advice: Gain Weight. After fifty pounds, the good guys won't see you, and after a hundred or so, even heat-seeking missiles will pass you right by. The bigger you get, the less substance you have, until you're constructed almost entirely of air.

But despite the potential it offers for stealth, small-scale espionage, and wealth beyond my wildest dreams, invisibility has a down side which, in my experience, outweighs its benefits a thousand to one. Ask about any period of my life (after about age nine, when I first became fat) and from it I'll recall a story illustrating the god-awfulness of being translucent. Take, for instance, junior high school, that pit of despair within which, admittedly, everyone rolled around in fetal position; it's just that not everyone had to do it so *imperceptibly:* Pretty girls got to have crying fits (tantrums), and pretty boys got to have fistfights (tantrums), each of them surrounded by groups of adoring fans. The fat and the ugly (widely believed to be the same thing) got to wail alone into their pillows.

Those years, if one could not be popular oneself, one held tight to the cheerleading raiment of those who *were* popular, hoping that some of Perfect Patty's leftover desirability would fall upon one's own garments like dandruff. My popularity-by-association strategy was to become the ideal confidante, the secret confessor to whom each budding prom queen would whisper, "I can't talk to anyone else about this"—*this* being most often characterized by fear: of competition, of losing her winnings, of sex and self and solitariness.

So the Shining Ones talked to me, sharing their angst during long and poetic late-night meetings which in themselves were an education in compassion and in the ways people are so alike at the core. I could not have named, at the time, why the listening act was so painful—to hear and then answer back is not, on the whole, a strenuous endeavor—but I have the vocabulary now to dissect those moments, to lift aside their cool surfaces and probe the well-preserved subtexts underneath. What I observe makes me sad even today, because it exposes, finally, the overarching falsehood of those times, the comforting myth I so willfully believed: that while speaking earnestly toward my face, Perfect Patty (and Mindy, and Sue) ultimately *saw* me there inside my body, identified me as substantial, coequal, real. I believed, in short, that they loved me—which they may have, but not as a peer for whom one might arrange a boyfriend or a jury-approved dress for homecoming. No, I was more a beloved pet, a sin-eater, a mother even—a spacious void into which these young women could speak; I would never be a competitor (I didn't even have the ball field's address), and therefore was not—as was the concrete segment of the populace—to be feared.

I remember discovering, during this period, that boys also craved a listening ear, and while I did cultivate these attachments (one must solicit male attention at any price) I also understood the nature—not just after the fact, but even then—of the small, steady ache in my chest. Truthfully, it required no great insight to interpret statements like "Girls are so hard to talk to, I can never say anything important" as "I can talk to you, but then you aren't officially a girl," and I want to time-travel back to slap myself, to scream, "What is WRONG with you, that you let people look THROUGH you like this?" Then again, I know what my teen self would say, that her choices were to sit murmuring into the phone ("Mm-hmm, I know just what you mean"), or to have no human contact at all, for who would think to party with a person who was neither tangible *nor* more audible than the breath from one's own lungs?

And of course, here in adulthood not much has changed. I and my larger friends swap stories of indignation, episodes where we find ourselves overlooked out there among the perceptible folk. One popular pastime among (visible) American women is to gather for a restaurant lunch and to discuss 1) the "badness" value of each menu item (avocados are "bad," meaning they are delicious but fattening; wheatgrass is "good," i.e., revolting but completely noncaloric) and 2) the unspeakable things the "bad" foods will do to each assembled physique. Every fat woman I know has been present at one of these ceremonies and has remarked afterward upon the quickness of the thin participants to use vocabulary like "grossly fat," "massively huge," and "behemoth," even with a person fitting those descriptions seated right there at the table. A friend of mine once reached her limit after two hours of hearing her divorced lunch companions discussing their diets and workout routines. When one of the divorcées pinched her abdomen and said, "No man is ever going to look at me, I've got to work harder on these abs," my (round in the middle) friend asked, "So would you say I don't stand a chance, myself?" The abs woman looked at her like she'd just materialized from the ether (as, in a sense, she had), answering after a moment, "I didn't realize you were interested in dating," no doubt having made this judgment based upon the flabby nature of my friend's upper arms (and legs, torso, etc.). The assumption was that if my friend wanted men to *see* her, then surely she would make her body *smaller*.

To be sure, on occasion these antifat comments are made pointedly, for the "benefit" of the obese girl at hand—sort of the way a parent says, in the presence of her teenager, "Boy, that must have been the best Mother's Day gift ever, when your daughter swept the garage." But very often I find that if I cough, in the middle of a cellulite-related discussion, and mention that I'm uncomfortable viewing my thighs as mortal enemies, the immediate look I get from the thin women is blank—not guilty, not smug, but utterly blank—and then they jolt awake somehow, turn red, and say, "Oh, but I wasn't thinking of *you.*"

Which is, in fact, just the point. How often *do* we think of that which we cannot see? I guarantee that God himself would receive much greater notice if he strode in person through the employee lunch room; if nothing else, all heads would immediately bow in thanks for the tuna surprise on toast. Similarly, it's not always that a fat person's "spaciousness" commands *more* than its share of attention (observe that I say "not always" instead of "never"; I once had a new acquaintance of mine compliment me on my personality by saying, "The more I know you, the less I seem to notice your weight," to which I wish I had replied, "I know what you mean. I find myself paying less and less attention to your acne scars"); instead, that very trait of bigness somehow diffuses her presence until she becomes amorphous, a cipher, an indistinct aura in the room.

I know a woman who is lately becoming visible. After too many pulled tendons and wrenched muscles (she lives in the woods and hauls her own firewood, repairs her own log house, digs her own truck out of ditches), Jean has started a weight-lifting regimen and those achy-breaky body parts are beginning to toughen. She is also, somewhat coincidentally, becoming smaller, harder, more "buff." Occasionally now she is having experiences—at the gas pump, at the welding shop (yes, she aspires to learn to weld)—in which men strike up unnecessary conversations, the sort where they make actual eye contact and then talk about anything (car problems, national news items, whatever) that will prolong the moment. (As I understand it, strictly from hearsay, this is what is known as "checking someone out.") Jean says that the first time this happened to her, she honestly did the look-behind-you-to-see-who-else-is-there thing, and then nearly said to the guy, "Who are you talking to? You can't see me."

My first response to Jean's stories is something I would not have expected. Well, all right, my *very* first response is to hate her with all-consuming wrath, but after that I feel a little apprehensive, wondering how she will distinguish now between the nice guys and the creeps. If she is being sought after, if in her vicinity everyone wears only his best disposition, by what means will she discover who is genuinely kind? Being invisible, a fat person can act as her own surveillance camera, her own hidden-in-the-lampshade listening device. She sees—I see—people behaving as if they are entirely alone, picking their noses, adjusting their underwear, expressing themselves as racist, or egotistical, or insensitive and full of venom. If a man or woman is selfish, I will see this first, and if generous, I will see this also. Discernment is perhaps the one benefit (aside from the bank-robbery possibilities) of being fat in this world; but it is a benefit which gives me some version of safety; for although the villains are sometimes more villainous to me because of my size, at least I understand them to *be* the bad guys, and they cannot likely take me unawares.

Tight Fits

I. Unbuckled

Japan Airlines Flight 802 destination Bangkok International Airport begins to move out of O'Hare, and I sit unbuckled with the thought of the next twenty-one hours cramped in this 747. I sigh. My knees bounce. The seat has the texture of a potato sack, hard on the skin, irritating my neck and arms. Everything irritates me.

A flight attendant notices my dilemma, but confuses it for insubordination.

"Sir," she says, "we are about to take off. Please fasten your seat belt."

"I can't," I say. She hears *I won't.*

"Please sir, fasten your seat belt," she says again. "Federal regulations." She is already annoyed. When she frowns,

I see the cracks in her makeup, how the color of her face doesn't match her neckline. She is not a natural blond.

I show her how the ends of the belt fall short. "You see?"

"Oh," she says, smiles and moves on. What about federal regulations? What about airplane safety? What about my safety?

Usually before takeoff, I begin a ritual. I put my index fingers in my ears and begin to chew—wide, long, languid movements of the jaw. I have done this since I was three, my first of seven trips to Thailand. Back then, the other passengers smiled, thinking me cute. Now they stare, and when I see them staring—my fingers in my ears, my mouth moving—they abruptly turn away into their newspapers or books. But I don't care. Nothing is as horrible as your ears popping and all sound becoming wind. The rumble of the airplane is wind. Voices are wind. When my ears pop, I hear the insides of my body—the stomach rumble, the steady or sometimes unsteady heartbeat. Every sound my body makes is a complaint about my life. "Lose weight," says my tired heart. "Please, for all that is holy, lose weight." My stomach grumbles. "Two pork steaks? Come on, guy, I'm only one stomach." "Shut up," I tell my system, but when my ears pop, every cell is saying something.

Because I am unconnected, I don't know what to do. Put my hands on the belt, as if having them there means I am connected in some way, or do the ear thing? I do both—one hand on the belt, one finger in the ear, my mouth opening and closing. The plane tilts its nose up into the sky and I put both hands on the belt and chew vigorously. On the ground, I notice a multitude of golf courses—light green fairways, black lakes protecting putting surfaces, and sand traps that from above look like white dots. As the plane soars higher, I see another course, and then another. And then everything disappears under layers of clouds.

My ears pop. They always do. My entire body says, "Don't you wish you were down there, putting for a birdie, instead of up here, unbuckled?"

Travel tip for the overweight traveler: On the plane, if your waist size is larger than 48, before takeoff, ask a flight attendant for an extender. Extenders add an additional twenty inches to the seat belt and are an assurance of safety for larger travelers. Don't be shy. Be comfortable.

II. Pants

I am a tourist at the Temple of the Emerald Buddha, though I speak the language. My Nikon dangles around my neck; my hiker's backpack hangs loose on my shoulders; my eyes dart from one thing to another. My mother and her favorite sister, Aunt Jeeb, walk casually, uninterested, beside me. They are part of this world that I am not.

Before I enter through the temple gates, a guard stops

me. He shakes his head and points up and down at my legs. "No. No. No," he says.

I freeze. "What?" I ask.

"No. No. No. Hum sie gung gaegn ca san." *You can't wear shorts here.* He points in the opposite direction from the entrance to a long line of people, nearly all white, waiting to enter a large tent. They are all wearing shorts.

"Shit," I say.

In line, people enter the tent and emerge a minute later wearing long pants. It's like an assembly line for recalled dolls. You go in and then come out with the correct piece of clothing. It occurs to me, sweating in one-hundred-degree weather, wiping my forehead with a bandanna, that I'm fat, fatter than the usual tourist, fatter than the usual American. I'm over six feet tall, my waistline in the fifties. What can I possibly fit in?

When I walk in the tent, a little boy, about waist high, hands me a pair of light blue pants. I notice how small his hands are compared to mine, how they are bony and full of veins. Mine are plump. No veins. No bones, just fatty flesh. The boy grins like I am a private joke. "Big one," he says. He pats his flat stomach and arches his back, "Most big." Then he extends his arms out wide.

"Thanks," I say, wanting to put the pants over my head.

The pants feel light in my hand, a small crumpled lump, wrinkled and limp. I put them on in the dressing room, the pants hugging each thigh and stopping short at mid calf, my belly protruding over a six-sizes-too-small elastic waistband. I sigh because I can barely breathe. I walk out of the dressing room, embarrassed, the pants wedging up my ass and hugging my crotch. My mother hides her laughter with her right hand. Aunt Jeeb turns around quickly, and I see her body shake. Then she turns around with a wide grin that looks odd on her serious face.

"Look good," my mother says.

I frown, and they begin to laugh uncontrollably, bumping against each other.

Entering the temple grounds is like stepping through a portal into another world. I turn in slow circles and crane my neck to look at high steeples. My senses are overloaded. Everything hits me at once—golden spires, stone statues, and magnificent *yuks,* giants. The yuks stand guard at the entranceway, thirty feet tall with long swords held at rest in front of them. The tips of the swords point down, immense yuk hands on the jeweled hilts. Bull-like horns curve from yuk mouths up to beady round yuk eyes. Their ears are golden flames that look like the wings on Mercury's heels, and their faces are carved into an angry smile, faces that are green, red, white.

An American couple asks me if I can take their picture in front of the Phra Si Rattana Chedi, the Main Stupa. The man, Texas in body, Texas in accent, points to a cheap-looking camera and says, "Pic-ture." Then he waves his finger back and forth between him and his wife, whose face is shiny with sweat. She smiles at me and says how nice I am.

I know I should say a word of English to them, identify myself as an American, too. But I don't. I let the charade go on, bowing my head and saying "K, K." I used to do this often, pretending to be someone I'm not. At a Thai restaurant in Champaign, Illinois, the owner confused me with a regular who always brought his wife and kid. He started talking to me in Thai and told me how lonely he was, how he barely knew a word of English and how he could never leave the restaurant. He asked me how long I'd been in America and I told him ten years, instead of saying I was born here. He asked me what I did for a living. Import and exports, I told him. He asked whether I lived in Champaign so we could become friends. I told him no, I'm from Chicago, which is true. He gave me his card anyway and told me to give him a call whenever I was in town, whenever I came to visit my mother-in-law again. Bring the baby, he said, Allisara, a good Thai name.

The man points up, indicating he wants the whole Stupa in the picture. The Main Stupa looks like an inverted gold ice cream cone. The cone stretches far up into the sky, and I want to tell the couple that to get the whole cone in the picture I would have to be at the other end of the grounds; it is just too big. But I try my best. I aim the camera with one hand, making sure to get the embracing couple in the frame. I count with my other hand. On three, I take the picture.

"Thank you," the man says slowly.

I hand back the camera and bow my head. "S'ank you,"

I say. "S'ank you." The couple bows back, waving as they walk away.

My mother finds me near the stupa. "Now," she says, "Let me taking picture."

"No."

"Yes. So people seeing where you go in Thailand." She reaches for my camera, fingers lifting the straps over my head.

"Only half my body," I say.

"But gung gaegn look good." She puts the camera strap around her neck, smiling, showing off her white dentures.

"The pants look horrible," I say. "Half the body or no picture."

"K, K. Half."

I stand next to a gray stone statue of a Chinese warrior. He is about my height with small slanty eyes, chubby cheeks, and a long wavy mustache. "Look like twin," my mother says. The warrior smiles, as if he has done this be-fore, countless times, for other tourists.

My mother turns the lens on my camera, zooming in, I hope, on half my body. I remind her and she waves her hand, telling me she knows, she knows. She counts to three: *nungn, song, sarm.* Click. She stands up straight, proud of herself, letting the camera dangle at her stomach. "Good picture."

My mother says we should go and pay our respects to the Emerald Buddha in the Ordination Hall. Gold statues of Garuda, the Hindu God of Birds, and Naga, the King of Serpents, line the outside base of the hall. Garuda has Naga's serpentine body in his hands, spread wide like wings; his talons pin Naga to the ground, his face—half man, half bird—seems to grimace and smile at the same time. Paper signs flapping in the breeze with pictures of cameras and red slashes going through them are taped on various spots of the Ordination Hall. We drop off the camera and my backpack with Aunt Jeeb, who is now comfortably in the shade of a gazebo. My mother tells my aunt we'll pray extra for her. Aunt Jeeb nods and asks us to pray for lottery numbers.

Grabbing my hand, my mother yanks me to the front entrance of the temple, past tables of souvenirs—VHS and Beta tapes on the history of the Emerald Buddha in English, French, Dutch, German, Chinese, and Japanese; picture books; little Emerald Buddhas behind plastic encasings. My mother leads the way into the temple, visor still on her head, until she is asked in rough English by a guard to take it off. She apologizes in Thai, a little red with embarrassment, a little red with frustration for being confused as a foreigner, and continues to the front of the Ordination Hall. A Middle Eastern man, dressed in a bright, long white shirt that goes to the knees and a white turban, lays a white cloth as big as a bath mat on the temple floor. He kneels on the cloth and bows his head to the Emerald Buddha, praying loudly, arms and hands sprawled out in front of him. A white couple in matching tropical shirts stands in the very back of the temple. They do the sign of the cross and bow their heads, moving their lips silently.

My mother finds an open spot at the very front. She sits on her legs and folds her hands together. She elbows me to do the same. "Pray," she says. "Ask for good life, good afterlife, to be with me in next life, mama and son again. Ask to be skinny."

"You should ask to lose a couple pounds," I say, though she doesn't need to. I pray for what my mother tells me to, none of which sounds bad, though I do ask Buddha to give her less of an attitude in the next life.

I look up at the Emerald Buddha in his summer wear—a slinky gold suit of armor covering patches on his green chest. Each season in Thailand, the Emerald Buddha wears a different outfit. In the rainy season, his body is completely covered in a gold blanket. In the spring, the gold robe covers half his torso. In the summer, it's too hot for all that clothing. The Emerald Buddha sits on a gold-covered wooden throne made in the First Reign, 1782. He meditates, right hand over left, thumb tips touching. Like other statues of Buddha, his face is peaceful and serene, like someone high, his eyes barely open. And, of course, he is green.

My mother says for me to bow my head to the floor three times.

"I can't bend," I whisper. "These pants are too tight."

She tells me to do it anyway. "Praying no good if not. Buddha no hear."

"But—"

"Do it," she says out of the side of her mouth, eyes still closed.

I slowly lower my head to the ground, feeling the pants hug my bottom and stretch the seams. I hear the creak of threads. I pray to the Emerald Buddha again, asking him to hold my pants together, to not have the tourists behind me remember the fat man who split his pants and bared his ass in the Temple of the Emerald Buddha.

Travel tip for the overweight traveler: No matter how hot it is, and it is hot in Thailand regardless of the season, always wear pants when traveling to any temple. In Thailand, temples are regarded as sanctified places, and showing too much skin is a sign of disrespect to Buddha. T-shirts and flip-flops are also unacceptable. We suggest investing in light cotton polos and comfortable walking shoes. Buy zip-off pants that convert from shorts to long pants in seconds. To purchase these pants in your size, contact kingsizedirect.com or visit your local Big & Tall retailer.

III. On the mountain

I am sick. I feel nauseated. Uncle Taw drives up Suthep Mountain like a race-car driver, his 4 x 4 Montero weaving back and forth. He wears dark sunglasses on a cloudy day and black driving gloves. His shiny blue shirt is unbuttoned to mid chest. My mother says he looks like a gigolo.

Uncle Taw co-owns the hottest nightclub in Chiang Mai, Gigi's. He also owns a cheap hotel for backpackers. Today, he is in charge of my mother, my cousin Oil, and me. The ride to Wat Phrathat Doi Suthep, a temple on the mountain, is fifteen kilometers from the edge of Chiang Mai, or so it said at the base twenty minutes ago. The road curves and twists and we are taking turns too fast. Stop the car, I want to say. Please, I need to get out. But instead, I close my eyes and rest my head against the window. I fear that if I open my mouth something else will come out instead of words. My mother and Oil seem unaffected by the car ride. They tell me to look out the window, look at how high we are getting. I tell them to be quiet. I'm trying to sleep.

Just when I can't take it anymore, the car stops. Everything is still. "Tugn le lau?" I ask. *We're here?*

My uncle points up to the Golden Chedi, a gold cone much like the Main Stupa at the Temple of the Emerald Buddha. It towers above us on top of the mountain. "Dugn," he says. *Time to walk.* But Uncle Taw doesn't move. He leans against the Montero and presses buttons on his cell phone. My mother asks if he is coming up. He shakes his head and says he's been up there too many times. He says he'll wait for us down here.

This is my second time at Doi Suthep. When I was nine, my mother's whole family, all eight of her siblings, came to pay homage to the Chedi, which is believed to house one of Buddha's relics. Back then, to get to the top, there were two options: climb three hundred steps or ride up in something called a funicular car. Everyone chose to ride the car that clacked its way to the top. On this outing, however, there are no choices. Uncle Taw told us in the Montero that the funicular has been out of commission since the summer of 1997, when French tourists plummeted to their deaths. The workers who ran the car had taken out a vital piece of the vehicle because it made too much noise. That vital piece prevented the funicular from going backward. My mother said, "Oh, coan Thai," and shook her head. *Oh, Thai people.*

Even though I am still woozy, the stairs put a smile on my face. I feel like I have to prove something. The serpent heads on either side of the steps mock me, their bodies slithering to the top, a scaly handrail.

"Are you coming up?" I ask my mother.

She nods.

"Are you sure?"

The temperature is in the nineties, the sun hot on our backs. My mother is sixty-three, and as of late, has been complaining about being old. She has complained so much that her sisters tell her to shut up. They tell her, you can be old, but you don't have to act it.

"Yes," she says, then waves for me to go ahead.

I look at my cousin Oil, so thin, weighing ninety-eight pounds.

"Let's run up," I say.

"Bah lah?" *Are you crazy?*

I tell her we should do it for the exercise. She tells me to go ahead and exercise. I'm the one who needs to lose weight. She's going to take her time.

I keep the Golden Chedi in my sights as I start taking two steps at a time, my arms pumping, my breathing even. I feel good. I turn around for a second, on about step fifty, and look down. My mother and cousin make their way up at a slow and even pace. My mother looks at the ground while she climbs. My cousin talks to her, mouth moving rapidly. I turn and start my run again.

Fatigue first hits me in the chest. Then it wallops me in the gut, stealing my breath. I work harder for air. Fatigue begins to spread all over my body. My arms won't pump anymore. My legs are tight and heavy, weights tied to my ankles. My fat itches, around my thighs, all over my stomach and meaty back. I go up one step at a time, sometimes tripping because I don't raise my leg high enough. Then I stop to catch my breath, regain my lost energy. While I'm breathing, fatigue absorbs all moisture from my mouth.

I stop halfway up, hunched forward, using the handrail for support. There are lottery ticket sellers all along the steps up to the temple, strategically placed for weary climbers like me. I wish for water, not lottery tickets. One woman with black teeth wants me to buy a ticket from her. She has a small baby on her back. The baby looks at me, confused, probably never having seen someone as fat as me before, a yuk, probably wondering why I am making a lot of wind sounds. I think, How lucky you are, little baby, on your mother's back, snug and comfortable. Before I can catch my breath, my mother is at my side. She says she wants a ticket. My cousin wants one, too, perhaps more than one to increase her odds of being rich. This is my cue. I start running up again. The people going down are looking at me. A white man wearing a tan safari hat says, "Not much more to go." And there isn't much more, only about thirty steps, the Golden Chedi in my sights, getting bigger as I climb higher. I push myself to another level, where everything external vanishes—the tight thighs and calves, the heavy breathing, the sore back, the fat bouncing stomach. All my energy and thoughts are dedicated to getting to the top.

And I do it!

My heartbeat thunders in my chest, blending into one continuous thump in all the extremities of my body. I am light-headed. I lift my arms up over my head, stretching my torso, expanding my lungs for more air. I close my eyes, proud of myself.

A minute later, my mother and cousin reach the top. They are not huffing and puffing. My mother's face is red. Her forehead and temples are damp, but she doesn't seem tired. In fact, my mother is smiling, her chin up. I don't understand what I am feeling. On the one hand, I am so happy for my mother, astonished at her feat, her triumph over age. On the other hand, I feel a slight sting to my pride; my mother has accomplished the climb not so long after me without taking a deep breath.

My cousin buys three bottles of water. I chug mine down in three gulps. My mouth still feels dry, my tongue sticking to the roof, and it is hard to swallow. I steal my mother's water and finish it. She does not object. She says I should free some sparrows atop the mountain before making my rounds around the Chedi, where I will walk around the large golden structure three times with yellow candles, incense sticks, and a lotus bud between my folded hands.

On top of the mountain, the temple provides a beautiful panoramic view—to the south, the entire city of Chiang Mai; to the north, east, and west, lavender mountains. A young man walks around the perimeters of the temple with a six-foot stick draped across the top of his back and shoulders. At the ends of the stick are small cubical cages made of twigs and branches. My mother pays the man twenty baht and takes a cage off the end of the stick.

The three brown sparrows hardly move in the cage, their feathers poking out, and their small heads, streaked with gray and white lines, squat against their bodies. Two of the sparrows face the opening of the cage; one is squished in the middle facing the other direction. They hardly make a sound.

My mother hands me the cage. "Open," she says. "Make wish."

I pet the feathers along the side, so soft against my finger. I bring the cage close to my face and whistle to them. One attempts to shake like a wet dog, but decides the cage is too confining; its wing, instead, drapes its sibling. I close my eyes and think of my wish, repeating it in my mind: *I want to be skinny. I want to be skinny.*

When I slide the cage door open, the two sparrows facing the exit zoom out in a flurry of wings and song. They fly over the temple walls toward Chiang Mai, 3,000 feet below. The other bird lingers. It stretches its wings and neck. It turns slowly around and stares at the opening, as if unsure what it sees is real. The sparrow's chest puffs out. Then, finally, it flies out of the cage, in the opposite direction of its siblings, past the Golden Chedi, heading north. I watch my wish disappear on the sparrow's wings.

Travel tip for the overweight traveler: Much merit is obtained by freeing captive animals. Fish are released in temple ponds. Sometimes even turtles, shellfish, and eels are bought from markets and set free to save them from the wok. Birds, according to ancient folklore, are believed to be Buddha's taiwadas, angels. They fly to Buddha and whisper wishes in his ear. Many times in folklore, on their journey to heaven, they are captured by monkey-faced demons and stuffed into small cages. By releasing them, you are freeing the birds from captivity, and symbolically, from the bonds of the demons. The birds will bring you good fortune. Make your wish count.

CHERYL PECK

Queen of the Gym

It happened again this morning. I was sitting there half-naked on a bench when a fellow exerciser leaned over and said, "I just wanted to tell you—I admire you for coming here every day. You give me inspiration to keep coming myself."

"Here" is the gym.

I have become an inspirational goddess.

In a gym.

I grinned at the very image of it, myself: here is this woman who probably imagines herself to be overweight— or perhaps she is overweight, she is just not in my weight division—sitting on the edge of her bed in the morning, thinking to herself, "There is that woman at the gym who is twenty years older than I am and has three extra people tucked under her skin, and she manages to drag herself to the gym every day…"

It is not my goal here to be unkind to myself or to others. Perhaps I am an inspiration to her because I am easily three times her size and I take my clothes off in front of other women. Being fat and naked in front of other women is an act of courage. Perhaps my admirer did not realize that it was exactly when she spoke to me that I was artfully arranging my hairbrush and underwear and bodily potions to cut the buck-naked, ass-exposing mini-towel-hugging moments of my gym experience to the absolute minimum. She wears a pretty little lace-edged towel-thing to the shower and back. I don't, but I understand the desire.

It was not that long ago that she bent over to pick up something as Miss Tri Athlete walked into the locker room and whistled, "Boy did I get a moon!" Junior high gym, revisited: I can't swear that particular exchange was the reason, but I did not see my admirer again for the next month. To Miss Tri Athlete she answered, "Just when I had forgotten for half a second that I was totally naked…" I doubt that she forgets that often. Almost none of us do.

Nor do I: which is why, the first time someone in the locker room said to me, "I have to give you credit just for coming here," I smiled politely and thought ugly thoughts for some time afterwards. *Up yours* thrummed through my mind. *Nobody asked you for credit* zinged along on its tail, followed closely by *Who died and left you queen of the gym?*

"Like it takes any more for me to go the gym than it does any other woman there," I seethed to my Beloved.

"Well it does," my Beloved returned sedately, "and you know it. How many other women our size have you seen at our gym?"

The answer is—none.

There are women of all shapes and sizes—up to a point—from Miss Tri Athlete, who runs in the 20–25-year-old pack, wears Victoria's Secret underthings and is self-effacing about her own physical prowess to women who are probably in their sixties, perhaps even seventies. There are chubby women and postpartum moms and stocky women and lumpy women…but there are very few truly fat women.

Exercise, you might advise me solemnly, is hard for fat women.

Exercise is hard for everyone.

Exercise is as hard as you make it.

Miss Tri Athlete shared a conversation with me the other morning. She said, "It feels really good to get this out of the way first thing in the morning, doesn't it? I think when you plan to exercise in the evening it just hangs over you like a bad cloud all day." She can't be more than twenty-five, she can't be carrying more than six ounces of unnecessary body fat and I've never seen her move like anything hurts. Her joints don't creak. Her back doesn't ache. She sweats and turns pink just like everybody else. She trains like an iron woman, but she's relieved when it's over.

I don't believe it's exercise that keeps fat women out of the gym. I think it's the distance from the bench in front of the locker to the shower and back. I think it's years and years of standing in grocery lines and idly staring at the anorexic women on the cover of *Cosmo*, I think it's four-year-olds in restaurants who stage-whisper, "Mommy— look at that FAT lady," I think it's years of watching American films where famous actresses never have pimples on their butts or stretch marks where they had kids. It's *Baywatch*. Barbie. It's never really understanding, in our gut, that if we could ask her even Barbie could tell us exactly what is wrong with her body. And we all know, intellectu-ally, of course, that Barbie's legs are too long, her waist is too short, her boobs are too big and her feet are ridiculous, but she's a doll. What we do not know, as women, is that my sports physiologist, who is in her late twenties and runs marathons, also has tendonitis in her shoulder, a bad back, and passes out if she trains too hard. My former coach for the Nautilus machines had MS. None of us have perfect bodies. If we did have perfect bodies, we would still believe we are too short or too fat or too skinny or not tan enough.

None of us have ever been taught to admire the bodies we have.

And nothing reminds us of our personal imperfections like taking off our clothes. Imagining that—for whatever reason—other people are looking at us.

My sports physiologist is more afraid of wounding me than I am of being wounded. The program she has set up

for me to regain my youthful vim and vigor is appropriately hard. Not too hard, not too easy. It's just exercise. The
most difficult part of my routine, designed by my physiologist, is walking through the heavy-duty weight room to
get the equipment I need for my sit-ups. The weight room
is full mostly of men. Lifting weights. Not one of them has
ever been rude to me, not one of them has even given me
an unkind glance: still, the irony that I make the greatest
emotional sacrifice to do the exercise I like the least is born
again each time I walk into the room.

Someone might laugh at me.

Someone might say, "What are you doing here?"

I have a perfectly acceptable answer.

I joined the gym because my girlfriend said, "I want to
walk the Appalachian Trail." I have no desire to backpack
across the wilderness: but I could barely keep up with her
when she made this pronouncement, and I could see myself falling farther and farther behind if I stayed home
while she trained. I joined the gym because I used to work
out and I used to feel better. Moved better. Could tie my
shoes. I joined the gym because I dropped a piece of paper
on the floor of my friend's car and I could not reach down
and pick it up. I joined the gym because I have a sedentary
job and a number of aches and pains and chronic miseries
that are the result of being over fifty and having a sedentary job. I joined the gym because my sister, who is
younger than I am and more fit, seriously hurt her back

picking up a case of pop. It could have been me. It probably should have been me.

I keep going back to the gym because I love endorphins. I love feeling stronger. More agile. I can tie my shoes without holding my breath. I can pick papers up off the car floor without having to wait until I get out of the car. I don't breathe quite as loudly. I have lost that doddering, uncertain old lady's walk that made strange teenaged boys try to hold doors or carry things for me.

I keep going back because I hate feeling helpless.

Years ago, a friend of mine convinced me to join Vic Tanney, a chain of gyms popular at the time. There was a brand-new gym just around the corner from where we lived—just a matter of a few blocks. She had belonged to Vic Tanney before, so she guided me through the guided tour, offering me bits of advice and expertise along the way....I plopped down money, she plopped down money, and a few days later it was time for us to go to the gym.

She couldn't go.

She was fat.

Losing weight had been her expressed goal when she joined: now she couldn't go until she was "thinner."

Everyone else at the gym, she said, was buff and golden.

"I'll be there," I pointed out (for I have never been a small woman).

She couldn't go. She was too fat.

She was a size twelve.

I have determined that I don't particularly mind being the queen of my gym. There may indeed be women who wake up in the morning and sit on the edges of their beds and think to themselves, "There is that fat woman at my gym who goes almost every day, and if she can do it…" I am proud to be an inspirational goddess. It has taken me most of my life to understand that what we see, when we look at another person, may reflect absolutely nothing about how they see themselves. Always having been a woman of size, I have always believed that it must be just a wonderful experience to be thin. What I am learning is that the reverse of the old truism is equally true: inside every thin woman there is a fat woman just waiting to jump out.

We give that woman entirely too much power over our lives.

We all do.

Sympathetic Pregnancies

1.

During the nine months my wife was pregnant with our first child, I gained twenty-five pounds. After he was born, I didn't lose the weight and actually gained twenty-five more pounds during my wife's pregnancy with our second son five years later. I like to think of it as sympathetic pregnancy, my body so in synch with my wife's that I matched her transformation pound for pound. My empathetic sensibilities did not extend, thank goodness, as they sometimes do to experiencing a parallel brace of Braxton-Hicks contractions or a bout of morning sickness. It might be that I lacked the imagination to actually rewire my body's endocrine system to that degree of reproductive fidelity. I simply grew.

The weight did settle on my belly. As my wife grew rounder so did I. I suffered only friends and family, even while they admired and approved of the sensual fleshing-out of my wife, aghast at my own transforming body. "Oh that," I said, *"The Couvade,"* invoking the French for the phenomenon in order to (what?) make the weight gain arty or legitimate or scientific or, at the very least, explainable.

Couvade translates as the "hatching" or "nesting" and was first applied by anthropologists upon discovering cultures where husbands performed ritual renditions of labor in their own dedicated hut while their wives wailed for real in a hut next door.

It helped to bring up sympathetic labor as the reason for what was happening to me, to my body. We like to believe that we have control over our bodies and for the most part we do. We control our bodily functions, command sleep, order movement. To exercise is to take one's body for a walk. But pregnancy puts a lie to such a neat hierarchy of control. In pregnancy the body takes you for a ride. You are at the mercy of the chemical equations coursing furiously through the body. The body's biological imperative. The physical results are stunning, sudden, and miraculous. Of course that is to say the "you" to whom the hijacking of pregnancy happens is not every "you." It couldn't *really* happen to me. I could only witness this metamorphosis. And, I guess, while witnessing, I wished to let myself go, to let my body go. Three-fourths of a year when new life is imminent allows the old life to be in abeyance. I let go without knowing I let myself go. I like to think I allowed my body to surprise me with my own generative process.

But I believe my body did this on its own. The surprise was real.

2.

The cravings were real but not at all original. Not pickles but ice cream. That fall we drove to Davis Square and Dave's Ice Cream and ordered dishes and cones of scoops and dips after test-tasting the new flavors, working our way through the tubs in the glassed-in frozen cases, collecting the tiny plastic spoons like charms. We drove to Harvard Square that fall, to Herrell's who was also Dave but when he sold Dave's signed an agreement to stay out of the ice-cream business. Dave loopholed his way back into the business on the strength of his family name. We were in a family way and craved ice cream. We craved chocolate ice cream, the subspecies of which (Dutch Chocolate, Belgian, Chocolate Fudge, Brownie, Chip, Double Chocolate, Mousse, White, Dark, Chocolate Chocolate Chip, Chunked, Cookie-ed, Malted, Marbled, Mandarined, Mocha-ed, Minted, Plain) were as numerous as the other individual varieties found in the rest of the flavor spectrum. That fall we drove to Central Square and ordered ice cream at Toscanini's, asked that the various candies and cookies and fruit and nuts be mixed into our choice, folded together on a refrigerated marble slab. It looked, as the mixing commenced, as if the ice cream was consuming its ingredients, an enriching metabolism. We brought home

pints and gallons of ice cream and didn't bother to decant
the contents but spooned the confection directly from the
container, producing deftly curling glazed and glistening
waves of frozen ribbons rolling up into our mouths.

I marveled at the sculptural suggestiveness of this
media. I loved how the shop scoops welded together. The
balled ice cream towered, mounded, slumped into Willen-
dorf Venuses atop a cone, how that hood ornament of ice
cream modeled the rounded belly, breasts, and hips of a
pregnant woman. Ice cream could be sculpted into bodies,
and ice cream sculpted the bodies that consumed it. It layered and larded the articulated underlying skeleton. That
fall, the fall of ice cream, under its influence and in its
hands, we became these spherical corpulent snow people,
artist's models. That fall our bodies bulged and bubbled.
We became these B-shaped beings.

3.

The story goes that my father, born at home, was
thought to be, until the actual labor and delivery, a tumor.
My grandmother, fearing the growth was a growth, ignored
the symptoms in order to ignore the expected diagnosis,
steered clear of doctors, denial being the only remedy she
believed available to her. One hears of things like that happening, variations on a theme. The obese woman whose
massive body masks to her and the world this other body
swaddled within. And then there are the tumors that are, in

fact, tumors, but tumors masquerading as bodies. They are themselves the remains of other bodies of cells commencing on a reproductive journey only to lose interest—hair balls, sets of teeth or even the mummified ghost of a fetal twin absorbed by the other in the womb, pregnant pregnancy, nesting nesting dolls. The belly and the womb may become confused. The swelling of one by all appearances identical to the other. There is the impolite inquiry of the heavy woman as to her due date. A man's beer gut distends in meticulous imitation or vice versa. And there is a further variation of our discomfort in our own skin. Shame, embarrassment, blush—this burning blindness of the body and its costume of skin. You hear of the impromptu birth in the high school locker room, the bathroom at the prom. The student who abandons her baby after a full term of concealment. No one, when interrogated in retrospect, suspected, the complete camouflage of the body by the body. No one was able to distinguish the metamorphic growth spurts of an adolescent from those spawned by the spawn within. The body is so much about the Body. It grows, and it grows.

4.

I do not faint at the sight of blood. I do faint at the mention of the word *blood*. It has to do with the vagus, that vagabond cranial nerve that wanders down the neck and thorax and on into the belly. It is the conduit for sensation in a part of the inner ear, the tongue, the larynx, and pharynx and motors the vocal chords while it stimulates secretions to the gut and thoracic viscera. My friend Dr. Valerie Berry called it "one very interesting piece of linguini." An overactive noodle can send the pulse racing and the blood pressure crashing, the electric schematic of sympathetic suggestion. In an instant the blood rushes to my feet, my wiring for some reason shorting out with this outsized response. I'm sensitive. To what? To words. I weathered the witnessing of the births of my two sons attending the attendant fluids, flesh, and surgery. But merely typing the above, thoracic viscera, had me going. I think it is the Latinates, the antique Greek, that medicine employs to sound disinterested that tweaks my vagal response. Doctors have this desire to explain, to render in that dispassionate vocabulary the description of the body. It backfires with me. Laceration for cut. Contusion for bruise. Hemorrhage. I'm more comfortable with bleeding. The impasse that necessitated my first son's birth by cesarean section was described as cephalo-pelvic disproportion. My heart, *cardia,* skips a beat, arrhythmic. These words for me are engorged, obese with what? Meaning? No, more than meaning. They are viral. They get under my skin, into my system. The codes wired into language still thrill my own harmonic neural strings.

I will tell you a secret. In college I wrote my stories and poems in the medical library, and between insights or inspiration, I sacked the stacks, looking for anatomies and dissection manuals, diagnostics and the casebook descriptions of diseases to read. They would produce in me when I read them a kind of high. These simple combinations of letters, of words, of sentences sparked a collapse of my involuntary systems and, in fact, revealed the existence of those invisible involuntary systems by this very intimate disabling. Mere words could do that. Make me sweat, pale, lose consciousness, collapse. The words about the body took on body. Words were impregnated with meaning, with power. Words have mass, weight, density, gravity. Words have a physics all their own—bodies in motion, bodies at rest.

5.

She could keep nothing down. The paradox of morning sickness. Without ingesting any food she grew larger. The logic of dieting was busted. She busted open. The body reworked the material on hand, stored in a snub to entropy, a conservation of matter and energy. This was spontaneous generation. She was sick to death and brimming with health.

There was the time during her pregnancy where she could only stomach white food, beige food at best. Yogurt, rice, mashed potatoes, and oatmeal. As I remember this now, it seems I spent forever making oatmeal in the mornings so that she could get out of bed. I became attuned to the amount of water I added, the amount of time it took to boil. The consistency of the final gruel seemed vital.

Too runny or too stiff would trigger another round of de-
bilitating nausea. I was Goldilocks daily searching for this
mean, obsessed with food that finally in the fairy tale
seemed disconnected from nutrition, diet, weight gained or
lost. I remember trying to secret a few raisins, disguised as
lumpy clots of cereal, dusting them with camouflaging nut-
meg or cinnamon that only initiated in her a gag reflex and
revulsion. I finished up the starchy intolerable repasts,
thinking I shouldn't let this go to waste, standing before
the sink, the stove with a bowl and spoon, eating whitely.

6.

There is so much we don't know about pregnancy. For
instance, the reasons my wife lost two before the first baby
was born and then lost two more before the second. At the
time all the doctors vaguely indicated not to worry until the
third miscarriage in a row, citing the hopeful notion of diagnostic drift to explain their nonchalance. They figured
that miscarriages had been happening with similar fre-
quency and number for all of human history; it's just that
now our diagnostic tools were better able to record it. No
worry. Come back if it happens again, we were told. The
drift of such drift, however, becomes its own explanation.
Miscarriages go unexamined—no longitudinal studies, no
clinical analyses. Mothers who want to pursue the causes,
of course, lose interest when the next pregnancy takes and

goes to term, any study of past outcomes forgotten in the time-consumed present moment. We forget to remember. So no one knows. It's a mystery.

All her life my wife has dreamed this rather common dream. She is falling. As she falls she thinks that she is falling and that she is going to die. She plummets, closes on the ground. And then wakes up. Sleeping after she delivered her first baby, she had the dream. She was falling. But this time, as she fell, she didn't think while she was falling that she was going to die. As she fell in her dream, she thought: "Who is going to take care of my baby?" Poets are drawn to a word like *cleave*, a word that contains a meaning and simultaneously its opposite meaning. My wife is a poet. Birth is a cleaving and a cleaving.

After the third miscarriage my wife asked the young athletic attending physician when she could start up again. The doctor, perhaps distracted by her charting, perhaps simply self-absorbed, answered that my wife could resume exercise in a few days, later today if the signs indicated. Had we interrupted, with our emergency, this doctor's daily jog, her own regimen of working out? She was wearing running shoes, her hair tied back, sweats. Was she assessing my wife's bulked-up body differently now that the body was no longer bulk for a purpose, was no longer pregnant? Time to get back into shape. Into shape. As the saying goes you can't be half pregnant. My wife in an instant had become out of shape. The doctor had misunderstood. My wife was asking how long before we could start again to have sex, to make a baby, to be pregnant. She wanted to get back into that shape.

7.

We took pictures. A few days before she was due, she took off her clothes and posed in our sunny living room. There is an extremity to the nakedness during labor. The clothing of modesty is readily shed. The staged renditions of the moment on television and in movies are hilarious with their persnickety management of drapery and screens. We are all born naked. My wife had back labor and for a while a warm compress on her lower spine helped relieve the pain. Until it didn't. She had dilated, was in the part of labor called transition. She had changed. I applied the heated towel again. "What are you doing?" she screamed. "It feels like you are ripping off my skin!" This nakedness was beyond skin deep.

Back to the pictures, to the evidence of that body. We marvel still at its transformation. There is the apparent impossibility of it. How could it possibly work? It is freakish in proportion and scale, gravity-defying and grave. There is a luxuriousness as well. The skin, yes, glows. The darker skin of the aureoles, the eyelids, the lips grow darker. On the center line of the belly a vertical line appears running from the sternum, circumventing the belly from pole to pole. The telltale sign of the stomach's rectus muscle's sep-

aration, split open like, well, ripe fruit. You can't help it—
all the clichés are true. The pregnant body is not a human
body any more but a metaphor for ripe, for full. My wife
no longer recognizes herself in the pictures. It was a
strange visitation, her body inhabited both by a new body
and this other body built to birth the baby. We look at the
pictures with nostalgia and anticipation.

8.

I found myself in a room with nine pregnant women.
All of the women were in the very late stages of their pregnancies and very late. Their deliveries past due, they waited
in this converted surgical recovery room for their labors to
commence. All of them were massive. Their shapeless hospital gowns taking on now the sweeping contours of their
swelling bellies and breasts amplified their heft by defining
it, the fabric stretched taut across the rounded middles.
They all were hugely uncomfortable, in pain, of course,
and in various postures of steepening agony—standing,
sitting, or splayed in a bed. They had all been induced, that
is to say the hormone Pitocin had been introduced into
their blood streams via an intravenous drip to spark their
bodies into productive contractions. And it was working in
spades. The spasms now slamming through them were
juiced by the chemical, boosted, turbo-charged. The kick
they were receiving packed a bigger wallop than if the
body had kicked off on the process of its own accord.

This was truly gut-wrenching, a doubled definition of "spike" of pain. Some were hooked up to monitors that spit out a graph-paper narrative, scored with these mountain ranges of ragged edges that finally climbed and climbed—no denouement but only the inked evidence of one endlessly upward-sloping excruciation.

I had been told to wait in the recovery room with nine women in the throes of labor by a distracted doctor at the main desk. My wife, on the verge of birthing her first son (birth imminent, the chart had read), stalled in the delivery during the final pushing. She had been whisked off to surgery for a c-section, leaving me alone in the birthing room with the beeping Plexiglas incubator warming up in the corner.

"What are you doing here?" an orderly asked as he wheeled in a bucket and mop to begin cleaning. I told him no one, in the haste to get to the operating room, had told me where to be, where to go. "Man, you can't be here," he said, "I've got to get this room ready for the next one. They're stacked up out there." So I drifted down to the desk and to the distracted doctor who told me to take a seat in the recovery room.

The women in the room began, in their individual expressions of pain, to come into a communal tune. Each whelp or moan began to synchronize, a kind of round harmony. The sound was transmitted around the room, an a cappella fugue of agony. The women peaked one after the other. The last one subsiding into a whimper just as the next reached a muscular grunt and growl. It was as if there were only one big contraction that oscillated around the room or that, in fact, the room itself rippled in one long ululation of a continuous sustained contraction. Nurses and midwives whispered to their laboring patients to "ride" the contraction, and the cacophony in the room had the orchestrated order of the squealing shriek of a train of roller-coaster cars. As each woman emerged from her most recent bout with her body, her body that now was not her body but possessed by these biological imperatives and hormonal accelerants that split open a body to expel another body, they each opened their eyes to see me sitting by the door. And as they focused on me, as they waited for the next spasm to grip them, I could tell they really, really didn't want me here.

9.

In high school health classes, it once was popular to have the students carry around, for days or weeks at a time, ten-pound bags of flour. The exercise was meant to simulate the weight of a newborn baby and the sustained lugging to condition the sexually active or soon-to-be sexually active teenager to the consequence of said sexual activity, pregnancy, and the consequence of the consequence, live birth. The flour bags would be hauled to classes, held while eating lunch, babysat in gym class. Some students even dressed their bags of flour or pretended to change the bag of flour's diaper, an apparent mass hysteria all to better imagine this potential semi-attached dependent human mass.

Ten pounds! It is interesting that birth announcement boilerplate contains a space for the newborn's weight. What other formal communication announces that information? Obituaries do not state that, at the time of death, the deceased tipped the scales at a svelte 185. Nor do wedding invitations report the fighting weight of the bride and groom. Perhaps there is just not that much to describe when we describe a baby, a baby so easily disguised as a bag of flour. We are left with the basics. Hair and eye color can change color and so such intelligence is rarely shared. The kid's size, the length and weight, is hardly static, and yet it is duly noted along with the name and the time and date of delivery into the world. Most likely we broadcast the heft of the infant because all through gestation it has been the focus, this hidden relentlessly growing thing, this curious expanding loaf, a kind of staple. The newborn remains pretty much that way for months outside the womb, a swaddled package. In short, the baby is an embodiment of human weight itself. It boils down to bulk. Ten pounds!

So after the birth of my sons, I gained a different kind of weight. Where my wife had come equipped with organic cavities to host the burgeoning other, I had to make do with these artificial blisters—the Snuglis, the papoose cradle boards, and canvas backpacks—girded to my body by contraptions of harness tack and strap. I had a baby sling, an ingenious device that looked and was worn like a Confederate soldier's bedroll. I draped it over one shoulder and it rode around the opposite hip, and then across the back. The sling was even made out of sturdy striped ticking and expanded like a kangaroo's pouch to allow the baby to ball up inside the enveloping folds. The tug of gravity then cinched tight, suspending the joey in this simulated womb. I could not resist rubbing this new belly of mine, massaging this living deadweight that only occasionally stretched, compressed beneath the smooth skin of fabric. How my body was contorted. And how I contorted my body simply to bear this childbearing. I discovered the shelves and hooks, the nooks and ledges of my anatomy to shift the baby about, not hot potato so much as a slippery, springy sack of spuds. My hips. My shoulders. My lap. My elbow's crook. Any port in a storm. I piggybacked. I made a swing of my distended arms. The baby rode my butt, my hands behind me, the laced fingers saddling his behind. I was, during the infancy, a declension of containment— hold, held, holding. Even when exhausted I could not shed this limp limpet. On my back. The baby bedded down on my front, bore down, bearing his full and concentrated weight asleep on my belly.

It isn't hard to make the leap. The literal weight that must be borne comes to stand, in a very solid way, for the metaphoric tare a parent incorporates. I was weighed down and weighed down. As a father I grew grosser by the day, by the ounce. I still carry those extra fifty pounds, the current weight of my younger son. I carry the mass equivalent in size to this other person still. I have no other explanation for it. Sympathetic, my own gravidity.

The Man Who Couldn't Stop Eating

A Roux-en-Y gastric-bypass operation is a radical procedure and the most drastic means available to lose weight. It is also the strangest operation I have ever participated in in surgery. It removes no disease, repairs no defect or injury. It is an operation that is intended to control a person's will—to manipulate a person's innards so that he will not overeat again. And it is soaring in popularity. Some 45,000 obesity patients had gastric-bypass surgery in the United States in 1999, and this number is on its way to doubling by 2003. Vincent Caselli was about to join them.

At 7:30 A.M. on September 13, 1999, an anesthesiologist and two orderlies brought Caselli (whose name has been changed) into the operating room where I and his attending surgeon awaited him. Caselli was fifty-four years

old, a heavy-machine operator and road construction contractor (he and his men had paved a rotary in my own
neighborhood), the son of Italian immigrants, a husband
of thirty-five years, and a father to three girls, all grown
now with children of their own. He also weighed four hundred and twenty-eight pounds, though he stood just five
feet seven inches tall, and he was miserable. Housebound,
his health failing, he no longer had anything resembling a
normal life.

For the very obese, general anesthesia alone is a dangerous undertaking; major abdominal surgery can easily become a disaster. Obesity substantially increases the risk of
respiratory failure, heart attacks, wound infections, her-
nias—almost every complication possible, including death.
Nevertheless, Dr. Sheldon Randall, the attending surgeon,
was relaxed—chatting with the nurses about their weekends,
reassuring Caselli that things would go fine—having done
more than a thousand of these operations. I, the assisting
resident, remained anxious. Watching Caselli struggle to shift
himself from the stretcher onto the operating table and then
stop halfway to catch his breath, I was afraid that he would
fall in between. Once he was on the table, his haunches
rolled off the sides, and I double-checked the padding that
protected him from the table's sharp edges. He was naked
except for his "universal"-size johnny, which covered him
like a napkin, and a nurse put a blanket over his lower body
for the sake of modesty. When we tried to lay him down, he
lost his breath and started to turn blue, and the anesthesiolo-

gist had to put him to sleep sitting up. Only with the breathing tube in place and a mechanical ventilator regulating his breathing were we able to lay him flat.

He was a mountain on the table. I am six feet two, but even with the table as low as it goes I had to stand on a step stool to operate; Dr. Randall stood on two stools stacked together. He nodded to me, and I cut down the middle of our patient's belly, through skin and then dense inches of glistening yellow fat. Inside his abdomen, his liver was streaked with fat, too, and his bowel was covered by a thick apron of it, but his stomach looked ordinary—a smooth, grayish-pink bag the size of two fists. We put metal retractors in place to hold the wound open and keep the liver and the slithering loops of bowel out of the way. Working elbow deep, we stapled his stomach down to the size of an ounce. Before the operation, it could accommodate a quart of food and drink; now it would hold no more than a shot glass. We then sewed the opening of this little pouch to a portion of bowel two feet past his duodenum—past the initial portion of the small bowel, where bile and pancreatic juices break food down. This was the bypass part of the operation, and it meant that what food the stomach could accommodate would be less readily absorbed.

The operation took us a little over two hours. Caselli was stable throughout, but his recovery was difficult. Patients are usually ready to go home three days after surgery; it was two days before Caselli even knew where he was. For twenty-four hours, his kidneys stopped working, and fluid built up in his lungs. He became delirious, seeing things on the walls, pulling off his oxygen mask, his chest leads for the monitors, even yanking out the IV in his arm. We were worried, and his wife and daughters were terrified, but gradually he pulled through.

By the third day after surgery, he was well enough to take sips of clear liquids (water, apple juice, ginger ale), up to one ounce every four hours. On my afternoon rounds, I asked him how the sips had gone down. "OK," he said. We began giving him four-ounce servings of Carnation Instant Breakfast for protein and modest calories. He could finish only half, and that took him an hour. It filled him up and, when it did, he felt a sharp, unpleasant pain. This was to be expected, Dr. Randall told him. It would be a few days before he was ready for solid food. But he was doing well. He no longer needed IV fluids. The pain from his wound was under control. And, after he'd had a short stay in a rehabilitation facility, we sent him home.

A couple of weeks later, I asked Dr. Randall how Caselli was getting on. "Just fine," the surgeon said. Although I had done a few of these cases with him, I had not seen how the patients progressed afterward. Would he really lose all that weight? I asked. And how much could he eat? Randall suggested that I see Caselli for myself. So one day that October, I gave him a call. He seemed happy to hear from me. "Come on by," he said. And after work that day, I did.

Vincent Caselli and his wife live in an unassuming salt-box house not far outside Boston. To get there, I took Route 1, past four Dunkin' Donuts, four pizzerias, three steak houses, two McDonald's, two Ground Rounds, a Taco Bell, a Friendly's, and an International House of Pancakes. (A familiar roadside vista, but that day it seemed a sad tour of our self-destructiveness.) I rang the doorbell, and a long minute passed. I heard a slow footfall coming toward the door, and Caselli, visibly winded, opened it. But he smiled broadly when he saw me, and gave my hand a warm squeeze. He led me—his hand on table, wall, door-jamb for support—to a seat at a breakfast table in his flowered-wallpaper kitchen.

I asked him how things were going. "Real good," he said. He had no more pain from the operation, the incision had healed, and, though it had been only three weeks, he'd already lost forty pounds. But, at three hundred and ninety, and still stretching his size 64 slacks and size XXXXXXL T-shirts (the largest he could find at the local big-and-tall store), he did not yet feel different. Sitting, he had to keep his legs apart to let his abdomen sag between them, and the weight of his body on the wooden chair forced him to shift every minute or two because his buttocks would fall asleep. Sweat rimmed the folds of his forehead and made his thin salt-and-pepper hair stick to his pate. His brown eyes were rheumy and had dark bags beneath them. He breathed with a disconcerting wheeze.

We talked about his arrival home from the hospital. The first solid food he had tried was a spoonful of scrambled eggs. Just that much made him so full it hurt, he said, really hurt, "like something was ripping," and he threw it back up. He was afraid that nothing solid would ever go down. But he gradually found that he could tolerate small amounts of soft foods—mashed potatoes, macaroni, even chicken if it was finely chopped and moist. Breads and dry meats, he found, got "stuck," and he'd have to put a finger down his throat and make himself vomit.

It troubled Caselli that things had come to this, but he had made peace with the need for it. "Last year or two, I'm in hell," he said. The battle had begun in his late twenties. "I always had some weight on me," he said. He was two hundred pounds at nineteen, when he married Teresa (as I'll call her), and a decade later he reached three hundred. He would diet and lose seventy-five pounds, then put a hundred back on. By 1985, he weighed four hundred pounds. On one diet, he got all the way down to a hundred and ninety. Then he shot back up again. "I must have gained and lost a thousand pounds," he told me. He developed high blood pressure, high cholesterol, and diabetes. His knees and his back ached all the time. He had only limited mobility. He used to get season tickets to Boston Bruins games, and go out regularly to the track at Seekonk every summer to see the auto racing. Years ago, he drove in races himself. Now he could barely walk to his pickup truck. He hadn't been on an airplane since 1983, and it had been two years since he had been to the second floor of his own house, because he couldn't negotiate the stairs. "Teresa bought a computer a year ago for her office upstairs, and I've never seen it," he told me. He had to move out of their bedroom, upstairs, to a small room off the kitchen. Unable to lie down, he had slept in a recliner ever since. Even so, he could doze only in snatches, because of sleep apnea, which is a common syndrome among the obese, thought to be related to excessive fat in the tongue and in the soft tissues of the upper airway. Every thirty minutes, his breathing would stop, and he'd wake up asphyxiating. He was perpetually exhausted.

There were other troubles, too, the kind that few people speak about. Good hygiene, he said, was nearly impossible. He could no longer stand up to urinate, and after moving his bowels he often had to shower in order to get clean. Skin folds would become chafed and red, and sometimes develop boils and infections. "Has it been a strain on your marriage?" I asked. "Sure," he said. "Sex life is nonexistent. I have real hopes for it." For him, though, the worst part was his diminishing ability to earn a livelihood.

Vincent Caselli's father had come to Boston from Italy in 1914 to work in construction. Before long, he had acquired five steam shovels and established his own firm. In the 1960s, Vince and his brother took over the business, and in 1979 Vince went into business for himself. He was skilled at operating heavy equipment—his specialty was running a Gradall, a thirty-ton, three-hundred-thousand-dollar hydraulic excavator—and he employed a team of men year-round to build roads and sidewalks. Eventually, he owned his own Gradall, a ten-wheel Mack dump truck, a backhoe, and a fleet of pickup trucks. But in the past three years he had become too big to operate the Gradall or keep up with the daily maintenance of the equipment. He had to run the business from his house, and pay others to do the heavy work; he enlisted a nephew to help manage the men and the contracts. Expenses rose, and because he could no longer make the rounds of city halls himself, he found contracts harder and harder to get. If it hadn't been for Teresa's job—she is the business manager for an assisted-living facility in Boston—they would have gone bankrupt.

Teresa, a pretty, freckled redhead (of, as it happens, fairly normal weight), had been pushing him for a long time to diet and exercise. He, too, wanted desperately to lose weight, but the task of controlling himself, day to day, meal to meal, seemed beyond him. "I'm a man of habits," he told me. "I'm very prone to habits." And eating, he said, was his worst habit. But, then, eating is everyone's habit. What was different about *his* habit? I asked. Well, the portions he took were too big, and he could never leave a crumb on his plate. If there was pasta left in the pot, he'd eat that, too. But why, I wanted to know. Was it just that he loved food? He pondered this question for a moment. It wasn't love, he decided. "Eating felt good instantaneously," he said, "but it only felt good instantaneously." Was it excessive hunger that drove him? "I was never hungry," he said.

As far as I could tell, Caselli ate for the same reasons that everyone eats: because food tasted good, because it was seven o'clock and time for dinner, because a nice meal had been set out on the table. And he stopped eating for the same reason everyone stops: because he was full and eating was no longer pleasurable. The main difference seemed to be that it took an unusual quantity of food to make him full. (He could eat a large pizza without blinking.) To lose weight, he faced the same difficult task that every dieter faces—to stop eating before he felt full, while the food still tasted good, and to exercise. These were things that he could do for a little while, and, with some reminding and coaching, for perhaps a bit longer, but they were not, he had found, things that he could do for long. "I am not strong," he said.

In early 1998, Caselli's internist sternly told him, "If you cannot take off this weight, we are going to have to do something drastic." And by this she meant surgery. She described the gastric-bypass operation to him and gave him Dr. Randall's number. To Caselli, it was out of the question. The idea of the procedure was troubling enough. No way could he put his business on hold for that. A year later, however, in the spring of 1999, he developed bad infections in both legs: as his weight increased, and varicosities appeared, the skin thinned and broke down, producing open, purulent ulcers. Despite fevers and searing pain, it

was only after persistent coaxing from his wife that he finally agreed to see his doctor. The doctor diagnosed a serious case of cellulitis, and he spent a week in the hospital
receiving intravenous antibiotics.

At the hospital, he was also given an ultrasound scan to
check for blood clots in his legs. Afterward, a radiologist
came to give him the results. "He says, 'You're a lucky
guy,'" Caselli recounted. "I say, 'Did I win the lottery?
Wha'd I do?' He says, 'You don't have blood clots, and I'm
really surprised.' He says, 'I don't mean to break your bubble, but a guy like you, in the situation you're in, the odds
are you're gonna have blood clots. That tells me you're a
pretty healthy guy'"—but only, he went on, if Caselli did
something about his weight.

A little later, the infectious-disease specialist came to
see him. The specialist removed his bandages, examined his
wounds, and wrapped them back up again. His legs were
getting better, he said. But then he added one more thing.
"'I'm going to tell you something,'" Caselli recalls the man
saying. "'I've been reading your whole file—where you
were, what you were, how you were. Now you're here and
this is what's going on. You take that weight off—and I'm
not telling you this to bust your ass, I'm *telling* you—you
take that weight off and you're a very healthy guy. Your
heart is good. Your lungs are good. You're strong.'

"I took that seriously," Caselli said. "You know, there
are two different doctors telling me this. They don't know
me other than what they're reading from their records.

They had no reason to tell me this. But they knew the weight was a problem. And if I could get it down..."

When he got home, he remained sick in bed for another two weeks. Meanwhile, his business collapsed. Contracts stopped coming in entirely, and he knew that when his men finished the existing jobs he would have to let them go. Teresa made an appointment for him to see Dr. Randall, and he went. Randall described the gastric-bypass operation and spoke with him frankly about the risks involved. There was a one-in-two-hundred chance of death and a one-in-ten chance of an untoward outcome, such as bleeding, infection, gastric ulceration, blood clots, or leakage into the abdomen. The doctor also told him that it would change how he ate forever. Unable to work, humiliated, ill, and in pain, Vincent Caselli decided that surgery was his only hope.

It is hard to contemplate the human appetite without wondering if we have any say over our lives at all. We believe in will—in the notion that we have a choice over such simple matters as whether to sit still or stand up, to talk or not talk, to have a slice of pie or not. Yet very few people, whether heavy or slim, can voluntarily reduce their weight for long. The history of weight-loss treatment is one of nearly unremitting failure. Whatever the regimen—liquid diets, high-protein diets, or grapefruit diets, the Zone, Atkins, or Dean Ornish diet—people lose weight quite readily, but they do not keep it off. A 1993 National Institutes of Health expert panel reviewed decades of diet studies and found that between 90 and 95 percent of people regained one-third to two-thirds of any weight lost within a year—and all of it within five years. Doctors have wired patients' jaws closed, inflated plastic balloons inside their stomachs, performed massive excisions of body fat, prescribed amphetamines and large amounts of thyroid hormone, even performed neurosurgery to destroy the hunger centers in the brain's hypothalamus—and still people do not keep the weight off. Jaw wiring, for example, can produce substantial weight loss, and patients who ask for the procedure are as motivated as they come; yet some still end up taking in enough liquid calories through their closed jaws to gain weight, and the others regain it once the wires are removed. We are a species that has evolved to survive starvation, not to resist abundance.

The one group of human beings that stands in exception to this doleful history of failure is, surprisingly, children. Nobody would argue that children have more self-control than adults; yet in four randomized studies of obese children between the ages of six and twelve, those who received simple behavioral teaching (weekly lessons for eight to twelve weeks, followed by monthly meetings for up to a year) ended up markedly less overweight ten years later than those who didn't; 30 percent were no longer obese. Apparently, children's appetites are malleable. Those of adults are not.

The revealing moment is the meal. There are at least two ways that humans can eat more than they ought to at a sitting. One is by eating slowly but steadily for far too long. This is what people with Prader-Willi syndrome do. Afflicted with a rare inherited dysfunction of the hypothalamus, they are incapable of experiencing satiety. And though they eat only half as quickly as most people, they do not stop. Unless their access to food is strictly controlled (some will eat garbage or pet food if they find nothing else), they become mortally obese.

The more common pattern, however, relies on rapid intake. Human beings are subject to what scientists call a "fat paradox." When food enters your stomach and duodenum (the upper portion of the small intestine), it triggers stretch receptors, protein receptors, and fat receptors that signal the hypothalamus to induce satiety. Nothing stimulates the reaction more quickly than fat. Even a small amount, once it reaches the duodenum, will cause a person to stop eating. Still we eat too much fat. How can this be? The reason is speed. It turns out that foods can trigger receptors in the mouth which get the hypothalamus to *accelerate* our intake—and, again, the most potent stimulant is fat. A little bit on the tongue, and the receptors push us to eat fast, before the gut signals shut us down. The tastier the food, the faster we eat—a phenomenon called "the appetizer effect." (This is accomplished, in case you were wondering, not by chewing faster but by chewing less. French researchers have discovered that, in order to eat more and eat it faster, people shorten their "chewing time"—they take fewer "chews per standard food unit" before swallowing. In other words, we gulp.)

Apparently, how heavy one becomes is determined, in part, by how the hypothalamus and the brain stem adjudicate the conflicting signals from the mouth and the gut. Some people feel full quite early in a meal; others, like Vincent Caselli, experience the appetizer effect for much longer. In the past several years, much has been discovered about the mechanisms of this control. We now know, for instance, that hormones, like leptin and neuropeptide Y, rise and fall with fat levels and adjust the appetite accordingly. But our knowledge of these mechanisms is still crude at best.

Consider a 1998 report concerning two men, "BR" and "RH," who suffered from profound amnesia. Like the protagonist in the movie *Memento*, they could carry on a coherent conversation with you, but, once they had been distracted, they recalled nothing from as recently as a minute before, not even that they were talking to you. (BR had had a bout of viral encephalitis; RH had had a severe seizure disorder for twenty years.) Paul Rozin, a professor of psychology at the University of Pennsylvania, thought of using them in an experiment that would explore the relationship between memory and eating. On three consecutive days, he and his team brought each subject his typical lunch (BR got meat loaf, barley soup, tomatoes, potatoes, beans, bread, butter, peaches, and tea; RH got veal parmigiana with pasta, string beans, juice, and apple crumb cake). Each day, BR ate all his lunch, and RH could not quite finish. Their plates were then taken away. Ten to thirty minutes later, the researchers would reappear with the same meal. "Here's lunch," they would announce. The men ate just as much as before. Another ten to thirty minutes later, the researchers again appeared with the same meal. "Here's lunch," they would say, and again the men would eat. On a couple of occasions, the researchers even offered RH a fourth lunch. Only then did he decline, saying that his "stomach was a little tight." Stomach stretch receptors weren't completely ineffectual. Yet, in the absence of a memory of having eaten, social context alone—someone walking in with lunch—was enough to re-create appetite.

You can imagine forces in the brain vying to make you feel hungry or full. You have mouth receptors, smell receptors, visions of tiramisu pushing one way and gut receptors another. You have leptins and neuropeptides saying you have either too much fat stored or too little. And you have your own social and personal sense of whether eating more is a good idea. If one mechanism is thrown out of whack, there's trouble.

Given the complexity of appetite and our imperfect understanding of it, we shouldn't be surprised that appetite-altering drugs have had only meager success in making people eat less. (The drug combination of fenfluramine and phentermine, or "fen-phen," had the most success, but it was linked to heart valve abnormalities and was withdrawn from the market.) University researchers and pharmaceutical companies are searching intensively for a drug that will effectively treat serious obesity. So far, no such drug exists. Nonetheless, one treatment has been found to be effective, and, oddly enough, it turns out to be an operation.

At my hospital, there is a recovery room nurse who is forty-eight years old and just over five feet tall, with boyish sandy hair and an almost athletic physique. Over coffee one day at the hospital café, not long after my visit with Vincent Caselli, she revealed that she once weighed more than two hundred and fifty pounds. Carla (as I'll call her) explained that she had had gastric-bypass surgery some fifteen years ago.

She had been obese since she was five years old. She started going on diets and taking diet pills—laxatives, diuretics, amphetamines—in junior high school. "It was never a problem losing weight," she said. "It was a problem keeping it off." She remembers how upset she was when, on a trip with friends to Disneyland, she found that she couldn't fit through the entrance turnstile. At the age of thirty-three, she reached two hundred and sixty-five pounds. One day, accompanying her partner, a physician, to a New Orleans medical convention, she found that she was too short of breath to walk down Bourbon Street. For the first time, she said, "I became fearful for my life—not just the quality of it but the longevity of it."

That was 1985. Doctors were experimenting with radical obesity surgery, but there was dwindling enthusiasm for it. Two operations had held considerable promise. One, known as jejuno-ileal bypass—in which nearly all the small intestine was bypassed, so that only a minimum amount of food could be absorbed—turned out to be killing people. The other, stomach stapling, was proving to lose its effectiveness over time; people tended to adapt to the tiny stomach, eating densely caloric foods more and more frequently.

Working in the hospital, however, Carla heard encouraging reports about the gastric-bypass operation—stomach stapling plus a rerouting of the intestine so that food bypassed only the first meter of small intestine. She knew that the data about its success was still sketchy and that other operations had failed, and she took a year to decide. But the more she gained, the more convinced she became that she had to take the chance. In May of 1986, she went ahead and had the surgery.

"For the first time in my life, I experienced fullness," she told me. Six months after the operation, she was down to a hundred and eighty-five pounds. Six months after that, she weighed a hundred and thirty pounds. She lost so much weight that she had to have surgery to remove the aprons of skin that hung from her belly and thighs down to her knees. She was unrecognizable to anyone who had

known her before, and even to herself. "I went to bars to
see if I could get picked up—and I did," she said. "I always
said no," she quickly added, laughing. "But I did it anyway."

The changes weren't just physical, though. She had
slowly found herself to have a profound and unfamiliar
sense of willpower over food. She no longer *had* to eat anything: "Whenever I eat, somewhere in the course of that
time I end up asking myself, 'Is this good for you? Are you
going to put on weight if you eat too much of this?' And I
can just stop." The feeling baffled her. She knew, intellectu-
ally, that the surgery was why she no longer ate as much as
she used to. Yet she felt as if she were choosing not to
do it.

Studies report this to be a typical experience of suc-
cessful gastric-bypass patients. "I do get hungry, but I tend
to think about it more," another woman who had had the
operation told me, and she described an internal dialogue
very much like Carla's: "I ask myself, 'Do I really need
this?' I watch myself." For many, this feeling of control extends beyond eating. They become more confident, even
assertive—sometimes to the point of conflict. Divorce
rates, for example, have been found to increase significantly after the surgery. Indeed, a few months after her
operation, Carla and her partner broke up.

Carla's dramatic weight loss has proved to be no aber-
ration. Published case series now show that most patients
undergoing gastric bypass lose at least two-thirds of their
excess weight (generally more than a hundred pounds)

within a year. They keep it off, too: ten-year follow-up studies find an average regain of only ten to twenty pounds. And the health benefits are striking: patients are less likely to have heart failure, asthma, or arthritis; most remarkable of all, 80 percent of those with diabetes are completely cured of it.

I stopped in to see Vincent Caselli one morning in January of 2000, about four months after his operation. He didn't quite spring to the door, but he wasn't winded this time. The bags under his eyes had shrunk. His face was more defined. Although his midriff was vast, it seemed smaller, less of a sack.

He told me that he weighed three hundred and forty-eight pounds—still far too much for a man who was only five feet seven inches tall, but ninety pounds less than he weighed on the operating table. And it had already made a difference in his life. Back in October, he told me, he missed his youngest daughter's wedding because he couldn't manage the walking required to get to the church. But by December he had lost enough weight to resume going to his East Dedham garage every morning. "Yesterday, I unloaded three tires off the truck," he said. "For me to do that three months ago? There's no way." He had climbed the stairs of his house for the first time since 1997. "One day around Christmastime, I say to myself, 'Let me try this, I gotta try this.' I went very slow, one foot at a time." The second floor was nearly unrecognizable to him. The bathroom had been renovated since he last saw it, and Teresa had, naturally, taken over the bedroom, including the closets. He would move back up eventually, he said, though it might be a while. He still had to sleep sitting up in a recliner, but he was sleeping in four-hour stretches now—"Thank God," he said. His diabetes was gone. And although he was still unable to stand up longer than twenty minutes, his leg ulcers were gone, too. He lifted his pants legs to show me. I noticed that he was wearing regular Red Wing work boots—in the past, he had to cut slits along the sides of his shoes in order to fit into them.

"I've got to lose at least another hundred pounds," he said. He wanted to be able to work, pick up his grandchildren, buy clothes off the rack at Filene's, go places without having to ask himself, "Are there stairs? Will I fit in the seats? Will I run out of breath?" He was still eating like a bird. The previous day, he'd had nothing all morning, a morsel of chicken with some cooked carrots and a small roast potato for lunch, and for dinner one fried shrimp, one teriyaki chicken strip, and two forkfuls of chicken-and-vegetable lo mein from a Chinese restaurant. He was starting up the business again, and, he told me, he'd gone out for a business lunch one day recently. It was at a new restaurant in Hyde Park—"beautiful," he said—and he couldn't help ordering a giant burger and a plate of fries. Just two bites into the burger, though, he had to stop. "One of the fellas says to me, 'Is that all you're going to eat?' And I say, 'I can't eat any more.' 'Really?' I say, 'Yeah, I can't eat any more. That's the truth.' "

I noticed, however, that the way he spoke about eating was not the way Carla had spoken. He did not speak of stopping because he wanted to. He spoke of stopping because he had to. You want to eat more, he explained, but "you start to get that feeling in your insides that one more bite is going to push you over the top." Still, he often took that bite. Overcome by waves of nausea, pain, and bloating—the so-called dumping syndrome—he'd have to vomit. If there was a way to eat more, he would. This scared him, he admitted. "It's not right," he said.

Three months later, in April, Vince invited me and my son to stop by his garage in East Dedham. Walker was four years old then and, as Vince remembered my once saying, fascinated with all things mechanical. So on my Saturday off, we went. As we pulled into the gravel lot, Walker was fairly zizzing with excitement. The garage was cavernous, barnlike, with a two-story garage door and metal walls painted yellow. Outside, it was an unusually warm spring morning, but inside the air was cool. Our footsteps echoed on the concrete floor. Vince and a buddy of his, a fellow heavy-equipment contractor I'll call Danny, were sitting on metal folding chairs in a sliver of sunlight, puffing fat Honduran cigars, silently enjoying the day. Both rose to greet us. Vince introduced me as "one of the doctors who did my stomach operation," and I introduced Walker, who shook hands all around but saw only the big trucks. Vince lifted him up into the driver's seat of a front-end loader backhoe in one corner of the garage and let him play with the knobs and controls. Then we went over to Vince's beloved Gradall, a handsome tank of a machine, wide as a county road, painted yield-sign yellow, with shiny black tires that came up to my chest and the name of his company emblazoned in curlicue script along its flanks. On the chassis, six feet off the ground, was a glass-enclosed cab and a thirty-foot telescoping boom on a three-hundred-and-sixty-degree swivel. We hoisted Walker up into the cab and he stood there awhile, high above us, pulling levers and pressing pedals, giddy and scared all at once.

I asked Vince how his business was going. Not well, he said. Except for a few jobs in late winter plowing snow for the city in his pickup truck, he had brought in no income since the previous August. He'd had to sell two of his three pickups, his Mack dump truck, and most of the small equipment for road building. Danny came to his defense. "Well, he's been out of action," he said. "And you see we're just coming into the summer season. It's a seasonal business." But we all knew that wasn't the issue.

Vince told me that he weighed about three hundred and twenty pounds. This was about thirty pounds less than when I had last seen him, and he was proud of that. "He don't eat," Danny said. "He eats half of what I eat." But Vince was still unable to climb up into the Gradall and operate it. And he was beginning to wonder whether that would ever change. The rate of weight loss was slowing down, and he noticed that he was able to eat more. Before, he could eat only a couple of bites of a burger, but now he could sometimes eat half of one. And he still found himself eating more than he could handle. "Last week, Danny and this other fellow, we had to do some business," he said. "We had Chinese food. Lots of days, I don't eat the right stuff—I try to do what I can do, but I ate a little bit too much. I had to bring Danny back to Boston College, and before I left the parking lot there I just couldn't take it anymore. I had to vomit.

"I'm finding that I'm getting back into that pattern where I've always got to eat," he went on. His gut still stopped him, but he was worried. What if one day it didn't? He had heard about people whose staples gave way, returning their stomach to its original size, or who managed to put the weight back on in some other way.

I tried to reassure him. I told him what I knew Dr. Randall had already told him during a recent appointment: that a small increase in the capacity of his stomach pouch was to be expected, and that what he was experiencing seemed normal. But could something worse happen? I didn't want to say.

Among the gastric-bypass patients I had talked with was a man whose story remains a warning and a mystery to me. He was forty-two years old, married, and had two daughters, both of whom were single mothers with babies and still lived at home, and he had been the senior computer-systems manager for a large local company. At the age of thirty-eight, he had had to retire and go on disability because his weight—which had been above three hundred pounds since high school—had increased to more than four hundred and fifty pounds and was causing unmanageable back pain. He was soon confined to his home. He could not walk half a block. He could stand for only brief periods. He went out, on average, once a week, usually for medical appointments. In December 1998, he had a gastric bypass. By June of the following year, he had lost a hundred pounds.

Then, as he put it, "I started eating again." Pizzas. Boxes of sugar cookies. Packages of doughnuts. He found it hard to say how, exactly. His stomach was still tiny and admitted only a small amount of food at a time, and he experienced the severe nausea and pain that gastric-bypass patients get whenever they eat sweet or rich things. Yet his drive was stronger than ever. "I'd eat right through pain—even to the point of throwing up," he told me. "If I threw up, it was just room for more. I would eat straight through the day." He did not pass a waking hour without eating something. "I'd just shut the bedroom door. The kids would be screaming. The babes would be crying. My wife would be at work. And I would be eating." His weight returned to four hundred and fifty pounds, and then more. The surgery had failed. And his life had been shrunk to the needs of pure appetite.

He is among the 5 to 20 percent of patients—the published reports conflict on the exact number—who regain weight despite gastric-bypass surgery. (When we spoke, he had recently submitted to another, more radical gastric bypass, in the desperate hope that something would work.) In these failures, one begins to grasp the depth of the power that one is up against. An operation that makes overeating both extremely difficult and extremely unpleasant—which, for more than 80 percent of patients, is finally sufficient to cause appetite to surrender and be transformed—can sometimes be defeated after all. Studies have yet to uncover a single consistent risk factor for this outcome. It could, apparently, happen to anyone.

Several months passed before I saw Vince Caselli again. Winter came, and I called him to see how he was doing. He said he was well, and I did not press for details. When we talked about getting together, though, he mentioned that it might be fun to go see a Boston Bruins game together, and my ears pricked up. Perhaps he *was* doing well.

A few days later, he picked me up at the hospital in his rumbling six-wheel Dodge Ram. For the first time since I'd met him, he looked almost small in that outsize truck. He was down to about two hundred and fifty pounds. "I'm still no Gregory Peck," he said, but he was now one of the crowd—chubby, in an ordinary way. The rolls beneath his chin were gone. His face had a shape. His middle no longer rested between his legs. And, almost a year and a half after the surgery, he was still losing weight. At the FleetCenter, where the Bruins play, he walked up the escalator without getting winded. Our tickets were taken at the gate— the Bruins were playing the Pittsburgh Penguins—and we walked through the turnstiles. Suddenly, he stopped. "Look at that," he exclaimed. "I went right through, no problem. I never would have made it through there before." It was the first time he'd gone to an event like this in years.

We took our seats about two dozen rows up from the ice, and he laughed a little about how easily he fit. The seats were as tight as coach class, but he was quite comfortable. (I, with my long legs, was the one who had trouble finding room.) Vince was right at home here. He had been a hockey fan his whole life, and could supply me with all the details: the Penguins' goalie Garth Snow was a local boy, from Wrentham, and a friend of one of Vince's cousins; Joe Thornton and Jason Allison were the Bruins' best forwards, but neither could hold a candle to the Penguins' Mario Lemieux. There were nearly twenty thousand people at the game, but within ten minutes Vince had found a friend from his barbershop sitting just a few rows away.

The Bruins won, and we left cheered and buzzing. Afterward, we went out to dinner at a grill near the hospital. Vince told me that his business was finally up and running. He could operate the Gradall without difficulty, and he'd had full-time Gradall work for the past three months. He was even thinking of buying a new model. At home, he had moved back upstairs. He and Teresa had taken a vacation in the Adirondacks; they were going out evenings, and visiting their grandchildren.

I asked him what had changed since I saw him the previous spring. He could not say precisely, but he gave me an example. "I used to love Italian cookies, and I still do," he said. A year ago, he would have eaten to the point of nausea. "But now they're, I don't know, they're too sweet. I eat one now, and after one or two bites I just don't want it." It was the same with pasta, which had always been a problem for him. "Now I can have a taste and I'm satisfied."

Partly, it appeared that his taste in food had changed. He pointed to the nachos and Buffalo wings and hamburgers on the menu, and said that, to his surprise, he no longer felt like eating any of them. "It seems like I lean toward protein and vegetables nowadays," he said, and he ordered a chicken Caesar salad. But he also no longer felt the need to stuff himself. "I used to be real reluctant to push food away," he told me. "Now it's just—it's different." But when did this happen? And how? He shook his head. "I wish I could pinpoint it for you," he said. He paused to consider. "As a human, you adjust to conditions. You don't think you are. But you are."

These days, it isn't the failure of obesity surgery that is prompting concerns but its success. For a long time it was something of a bastard child in respectable surgical circles. Bariatric surgeons—as obesity surgery specialists are called—faced widespread skepticism about the wisdom of forging ahead with such a radical operation when so many previous versions had failed, and there was sometimes fierce resistance to their even presenting their results at the top surgical conferences. They sensed the contempt other surgeons had for their patients (who were regarded as having an emotional, even moral, problem) and often for them.

This has all changed now. The American College of Surgeons recently recognized bariatric surgery as an accepted specialty. The National Institutes of Health issued a consensus statement endorsing gastric-bypass surgery as the only known effective therapy for morbid obesity, one able to produce long-term weight loss and improvement in health. And most insurers have agreed to pay for it.

Physicians have gone from scorning it to encouraging, sometimes imploring, their severely overweight patients to undergo a gastric-bypass operation. And that's not a small number of patients. More than five million adult Americans meet the strict definition of morbid obesity. (Their "body mass index"—that is, their weight in kilograms divided by the square of their height in meters—is forty or more, which for an average man is roughly a hundred pounds or more overweight.) Ten million more weigh just under the mark but may nevertheless have obesity-related health problems that are serious enough to warrant the surgery. There are ten times as many candidates for obesity surgery right now as there are for heart-bypass surgery in a year. So many patients are seeking the procedure that established surgeons cannot keep up with the demand. The American Society of Bariatric Surgery has only five hundred members nationwide who perform gastric-bypass operations, and their waiting lists are typically months long. Hence the too familiar troubles associated with new and lucrative surgical techniques (the fee can be as much as twenty thousand dollars): newcomers are stampeding to the field, including many who have proper training but have not yet mastered the procedure, and others who have no training at all. Complicating matters further, individual surgeons are promoting a slew of variations on the standard operation which haven't been fully researched—the "duodenal switch," the "long limb" bypass, the laparoscopic bypass. And a few surgeons are pursuing new populations, such as adolescents and people who are only moderately obese.

Perhaps what's most unsettling about the soaring popularity of gastric-bypass surgery, however, is simply the world that surrounds it. Ours is a culture in which fatness is seen as tantamount to failure, and get-thin-quick promises— whatever the risks—can have an irresistible allure. Doctors may recommend the operation out of concern for their patients' health, but the stigma of obesity is clearly what drives many patients to the operating room. "How can you let yourself look like that?" is often society's sneering, unspoken question, and sometimes its spoken one as well. (Caselli told me of strangers coming up to him on the street and asking him precisely this.) Women suffer even more than men from the social sanction, and it's no accident that seven times as many women as men have had the operation. (Women are only an eighth more likely to be obese.)

Indeed, deciding *not* to undergo the surgery, if you qualify, is at risk of being considered the unreasonable thing to do. A three-hundred-fifty-pound woman who did not want the operation told me of doctors browbeating her for her choice. And I have learned of at least one patient with heart disease being refused treatment by a doctor unless she had a gastric bypass. If you don't have the surgery, you will die, some doctors tell their patients. But we actually do not know this. Despite the striking improvements in weight and health, studies have not yet proved a corresponding reduction in mortality.

There are legitimate grounds for being wary of the procedure. As Paul Ernsberger, an obesity researcher at Case Western Reserve University, pointed out to me, many patients undergoing gastric bypass are in their twenties and thirties. "But is this really going to be effective and worthwhile over a forty-year span?" he asked. "No one can say." He was concerned about the possible long-term effects of nutritional deficiencies (for which patients are instructed to take a daily multivitamin). And he was concerned about evidence from rats that raises the possibility of an increased risk of bowel cancer.

We want progress in medicine to be clear and unequivocal, but of course it rarely is. Every new treatment has gaping unknowns—for both patients and society—and it can be hard to decide what to do about them. Perhaps a simpler, less radical operation will prove effective for obesity. Perhaps the long-sought satiety pill will be found. Nevertheless, the gastric bypass is the one thing we have now that works. Not all the questions have been answered, but there are more than a decade of studies behind it. And so we forge ahead. Hospitals everywhere are constructing obesity-surgery centers, ordering reinforced operating tables, training surgeons and staff. At the same time, everyone expects that, one day, something new and better will be discovered that will make what we're now doing obsolete.

Across from me, in our booth at the grill, Vince Caselli pushed his chicken Caesar salad aside only half eaten. "No taste for it," he said, and he told me he was grateful for that. He had no regrets about the operation. It had given him his life back, he said. But, after one more round of drinks and with the hour growing late, it was clear that he still felt uneasy.

"I had a serious problem and I had to take serious measures," he said. "I think I had the best technology that is available at this point. But I do get concerned: Is this going to last my whole life? Someday, am I going to be right back to square one—or worse?" He fell silent for a moment, gazing into his glass. Then he looked up, his eyes clear. "Well, that's the cards that God gave me. I can't worry about stuff I can't control."

Now You See Me,
Now You Don't

She glows at me on the computer screen—all 310 pounds of her. She smiles to me from the steps of the pyramids in El Salvador. She looks like my friends. She looks like people I have met that I wanted to get to know better. She is out—she is living her life.

I am reading her story, in her own words, on the weight-loss surgery Web site. Three words appear above her before and after pictures: "In Loving Memory." Had I not already known of her grievous surgical complications, I would have missed her death entirely. I would have thought she was alive and happy, as she appears in the photos. I would have expected her to be as vibrant as her words.

In 2001, just over a year after her surgery, she weighs 145 pounds. By 2002, she is dead.

She lived thirty-three years and six months. Today, as I

write this, I am thirty-three years and six months old. I breathe. I live. I am loved. I fell a week ago and skinned my knee. It hurts tonight and I know I am alive.

I read her words. Her first diet, at the age of seven. I understand—mine was at eight. I stopped dieting in college, but she kept trying. I went to law school. She tried more diets. She tried everything, even drugs—legal and otherwise. She always gained the weight back, plus some. I became a performer, placing my fat body onstage under bright lights where I could be seen. She shrunk from view. She writes, "I wanted to hide. I wanted to die." I bet she lowered her eyes when she walked past a mirror.

Her choice to have surgery was not impulsive. She researched the procedures. She met someone online who'd had a "good result" and liked the surgeon. Questioning whether she "really wanted to do something so drastic to herself," she shares with me her decision: "It didn't take long to answer the…question. I was so miserable that I thought, 'Being dead would be preferable to this. This isn't living.'" I know what she means, or rather, what she *meant*. At the age of ten I was so miserable, I made a bargain with myself: If I was still fat in five months, then I could commit suicide. I thought I was being generous by giving myself an extra shot at getting thin. We did not have the surgery then, just weight-loss camps and diet books.

It occurs to me that a person who feels it is better to be dead than to be fat may not be in the right frame of mind to think clearly about choosing weight-loss surgery, which

is estimated at $20,000 to $50,000 per patient. It also occurs to me that a medical professional who advises that
weight loss is worth almost any risk should not practice
medicine on living beings.

Despite promotional material claiming that new variations of these procedures have fewer complications, the
bariatric profession fails to maintain accurate, comprehen-
sive, long-term data on their survivors. This deficiency
speaks volumes about the integrity of the field. We do not
know what happens to the people who have these surger-
ies. Of course, the patients who do well are easy to see.
The people who have bad results, as fat as they are, they
slip through the cracks. They drop out of the studies. They
do not stay in touch with their surgeons. They disappear.
Sometimes they die.

It is a humid night. I am still looking at her picture on
the screen. Her hair is frizzy. So is mine. I never knew her
and now I never will. The last words from her that I will
ever read are illuminated at the bottom of the screen:
"[This is] the best choice I've ever made for myself. In
choosing [surgery], I chose life."

Diet plans and weight-loss products do not work, but
they do sell. To generate profits, marketers often employ
a rhetorical strategy called forced choice. By framing the
issues carefully, the manipulated person's options are
restricted, but their personal sense of autonomy is maintained. Sometimes this is a valid tactic. For example, rather
than ordering a child to hold your hand when crossing the

street, use forced choice. Ask them, "Do you want to hold my hand, or do you want to hold Aunt Sara's hand, when you cross the street?" In contrast, forced choice is not an ethically defensible strategy when the goal is to market a worthless weight-loss product, or to pressure someone into a risky surgery: "Do you want to have a date or be fat?" "Do you want to have a job or be fat?" "Do you want to be fit or be fat?" "Do you want to have a life or be fat?" In our culture these sentiments are repeated so many times that we have taken them to heart. We forget to step outside the box because we can no longer see it.

I frequently do diversity and legal trainings about weight. Recently I lectured at the Childhood Obesity Conference. It was held in Southern California where my mother lives, so I invited her to attend my talk. To begin examining our stereotypes about fat, I shared a personal anecdote:

During law school at UC Berkeley I kept myself human by volunteering on a fat women's zine. We were contacted by the Vegetarian Club at a Los Angeles college. They wanted to bring us down to have a campus-wide debate with them. The fat women versus the vegetarians! See the problem? Which side am I supposed to sit on since I have been a vegetarian since I was eleven? And that is the power of prejudice—it makes you act goofy. It blinds you to common sense. It makes you see things that are not there, like fat women madly sucking down piles of meat.

A health care provider came up after my talk. She said she enjoyed it, but she just wanted to check with me and confirm that I was not actually a vegetarian—that I was merely fictionalizing to make a point about stereotypes, which she assured me she understood. I told her the story was true and that I am a vegetarian. She could not believe me. She insisted that she understood the concept of tolerance, she promised that she would not tell anyone, but implored me to tell her "the truth"—she really needed to know. "OK, I will tell you the truth," I whispered covertly, "I really am a vegetarian. I have been since I was eleven." Dumbfounded and unconvinced, she could not accept what I was saying. She was not a bad person. She was simply a person laboring under a stereotype—one that had great power over her. Although I was thirty-one years old and a respected professional, although she knew I was not malicious, I finally had to introduce her to my mother so she could get the confirmation that she needed. It took the wills of three people to overcome this one quirky little stereotype—that fat people eat lots of meat and that thin people are vegetarians.

I am constantly amazed at our lack of creativity when it comes to stereotypes. Basically we pick from a short list: greedy, lazy, ugly, smelly, undesirable, deviant, voracious, disgusting, undisciplined, stupid, draining, sneaky, etc., and apply them in different combinations to whatever group is disfavored at the moment. African Americans, Mexican immigrants, Jews, welfare moms, queers, you name it—we just slap on the stereotypes, throw some stock footage up there (headless bellies and butts for fat stories, young men loitering by a housing project for stories on people of color), and you have "news."

I cannot talk about fat politics without exploring race, sex, and other forms of discrimination. For example, because there are more fat women than fat men and more fat African Americans and Latinos than fat white people, discrimination or harassment based on weight disproportionately impacts people of color and all women, where multiple characteristics combine to push them farther from the mainstream. A fat black woman may face discrimination that neither a fat white woman nor a thin black woman will encounter—that is the double whammy. Add on being queer or disabled and the bias increases exponentially.

Stereotypes repeated often enough mutate into cultural myths. The three most dangerous myths are: (1) fat is unhealthy, (2) fat is mutable, and (3) fat is unattractive.

Today we witness a concerted government effort to vilify fat. There is even a "war on fat" and, as it turns out, our country has a nasty little habit of declaring war before the evidence has come in.

Mainstream culture endlessly repeats the mantra "fat is

unhealthy." We must learn to educate ourselves and be savvy in our analysis. A lot of what is printed is untrue. The "300,000 deaths per year due to obesity" is a prime example of sloppy science. The figure was generated without regard to exercise and eating habits. Researchers and the media repeatedly confuse measures of fatness and measures of fitness. The Cooper Institute for Aerobics Research studied over 30,000 people and found that fat men who exercised regularly are almost three times more likely to avoid premature death than thin men who do not and that, when matched for fitness level, the longevity of fat and thin people is comparable.* If we are genuinely concerned about the health of fat people, then we should research how to make fat people healthier, not exclude fat people from health studies where weight loss is not the goal, as is the current norm.

Legally, one of the most serious misconceptions about weight is mutability—the notion that people are fat by choice and could therefore become thin people if they so chose. The average fat person may be able to lose weight temporarily, but there is no program, pill, or patch that will permanently turn the average fat person into a thin person. Weight-loss "failure" rates are astronomical: 90 to 98 percent. Even in-patient weight-loss programs have "failure"

*Blair, Steven, et al., "Physical Fitness, Mortality and Obesity," *International Journal of Obesity* 19, No. 4 (1995): S41–S44.

rates of 85 percent or more. But forget the figures for a minute, because it is just common sense. So many fat people want so desperately to lose weight permanently, that if it was doable, it would already have been done.

And while we are talking about weight-loss efforts, it is important to remember that attempting to lose weight can be harmful. In a 1950s wartime study by Ancel Keys at the University of Minnesota (which would be prohibited today because of the restrictions on human subject usage) researchers found that even men who were extraordinarily physically and psychologically healthy were significantly impacted by semistarvation. After only a six-month period of caloric restriction, marked personality changes occurred—one man even chopped off some fingers to get out of the study. Others obsessed about food, talking about recipes, smuggling food, and licking plates. Three changed their career plans and became chefs. Twenty percent suffered emotional distress so severe it interfered with their ability to function. All this with an average caloric intake of 1,670 calories per day!

Bizarre effects were seen upon refeeding. Some men ate till they vomited, and then ate more. Others felt hungry even after consuming 5,000 to 10,000 calories per day. The young men were irritable, depressed, and exhibited apathy toward starving people.

Though the myth of mutability is legally crucial, when it comes to daily quality of life, it is our narrow definition of beauty that is most limiting. The cultural myth that beauty equals leanness continues to disproportionately devastate our nation's adolescent girls and to limit all of our horizons, regardless of sex and age.

Beauty is a cultural creation. I enjoy pop culture, but I certainly acknowledge the fact that something, or more aptly, someone, is missing:

> Censorship! Censorship!...Look at what we don't see in magazines and on TV, except as butts of jokes. And such Big-butt jokes...Look at what's not there already....What don't you see? Twenty-eight percent. Twenty-eight percent of Americans. And we are big. So big we can't be seen.

Our popular culture creates a fiction about what is "normal" and what is "desirable." If a person is fat that individual is written out of the script, never to be seen.

And it gets worse. We, the Fat, are thankful for our banishment, forsaking the spotlight for obscurity and self-loathing. Many of us are so frightened that we do not want to be seen. We even choose not to see ourselves. We walk past mirrors with downcast eyes. We avoid photographs. We avoid crowds. We hide in our large clothes. We dream of being less, of being weightless.

We are not going to be seen until we first see ourselves. We must become grateful enough and rebellious enough to see our own beauty despite our culture. We must learn to see ourselves as worthy and valuable. We must become strong enough to defend this vision of ourselves.

Because I am a lawyer focusing on weight-related issues, people call me when their rights are violated. In the wake of the air terror of September 11, a profitable major airline began targeting fat passengers for discrimination. Stranded and harassed travelers contacted me while researching their rights. I studied the issues; the law is apathetic and the cases are rare. Finally, I learned of a promising lawsuit.

A New York drag performer was forced off an airplane by staff who allegedly said something like, "There's fat, then there's obese, then there's you." He did not merely take the abuse. He sued. I was tremendously excited to talk to him. I needed to hear about his case strategy, hoping that it would apply to the many new airline victims. On a personal level, I anticipated making a new friend. Using his size proudly as an asset onstage in his drag shows, he billed himself as the "Biggest Madonna." He was a master at "being seen" and he sounded really cool.

After the airline abuse, he disappeared from the spotlight completely. He began thinking people were laughing at him, not with him. He never took the stage again. I wonder if he started lowering his eyes when he passed a mirror.

Less than two years after the abuse, his lawsuit pending in court, he chose bariatric surgery. He died.

I face discrimination on the airplane. I get harassment on the street. I recognize it for what it is—intolerance. My body and mind are allies and refuse to be played against each other by internalizing that hatred. My own government has declared a war on fat, but I am at peace with my body. I choose to look myself in the eye when I pass a mirror. I choose life. I rejoice in being seen. No matter how hostile the climate, I will not disappear.

Fat Guys Kick Ass

That the world is run by fat guys is no secret (more on this later), yet Americans devote a tremendous amount of time, effort, and money to losing weight without ever stopping to consider the advantages of obesity. And the advantages are many—not least of which is that you can eat whatever you want.

I'm a fat guy—always have been. I'm not "big-boned" (surprise, there's no such thing), I don't "carry it well," and I'm neither "husky" nor "just a little heavy." There's nothing wrong with any of my glands. I'm not a victim in any way. I'm a fat guy because I eat too much. If I ate less, I'd lose weight. But I don't, because I love food (and I even eat food I don't love, because I love the mere act of eating). I'm a fat guy, as in I could lose 50 pounds and still be fat, as in I'm 5-foot-10 and 250 very apparent pounds (plus or minus 10 pounds depending on what I ate that day). I'm a fat guy, and I'm not alone.

According to a study published in the May 29, 1998, issue of *Science,* 54 percent of American adults (and 25 percent of children) are overweight (and that figure is likely skewed downwards by all the people who crash-diet the week before their annual physicals because they know they're going to get weighed). We, the fat, are the rapidly expanding majority. (The fat population has grown by 33 percent since 1978.) It is the thin who are abnormal.

I enjoy being a fat guy, although I must confess I wouldn't want to be a fat girl. The societal deck really is stacked against them (unfairly, I might add, because fat girls are in many ways superior to skinny ones). But being a fat guy is great. I've never felt that my weight kept me from getting a job or a girl, or from gaining admittance to a club. And it has many, many advantages.

Fat guys are strong. Ask any bar owner who hires bouncers, or anybody who gets in a lot of fights, or any high school wrestler. They'll all tell you the same thing: Don't fuck with fat guys.

Despite the propaganda of 10,000 suburban strip-mall tae kwon do "academies" and health-club self-defense classes, the simple truth is that victory in a fight is largely a matter of inertia. "The 300-pound tub-of-lard beats the 165-pound musclehead every time," says Navy Lieutenant Jonathan Shapiro, my brother-in-law and all-around physically fit tough guy, who spends much of his life recovering from various exercise-related injuries. "Fat guys kick ass."

In competitive wrestling, if one guy outweighs another by a few pounds, they put him in a different weight class— the match wouldn't even be fun. Every fat guy is inherently strong, but the ultimate weapon is the fat guy who knows how to fight (aka the sumo wrestler).

Fat guys aren't as slow as you think, either. I don't have time to explain all of Newtonian physics to you, but remember that a body in motion tends to remain in motion. Fat guys may have trouble turning on a dime, but they can move in one direction with great alacrity and effectiveness, as demonstrated repeatedly in every NFL game.

Still, the fat guy is essentially a peaceful creature. War is for the thin. Fighting requires effort, and minimum effort is the mantra of the fat guy. Efficiency and economy of movement are the fat guy's greatest allies. The thin think nothing of bounding up four flights of stairs, running to catch a bus, or invading a Caribbean nation, but fat guys plan their days around avoiding these very situations.

But they don't avoid dating. Dating is eating. Nearly every date centers around a meal, and fat guys are far and away the best dining companions. They are uninhibited eaters, they know all the best restaurants, and they know how to cook. Therefore, fat guys are the best dates.

The thin choose restaurants based on ambience; fat guys choose restaurants because the food is good. The thin may know how to operate a grill (badly) and make breakfast (badly), but every fat guy intuitively knows how to truss a capon, bake a wedding cake, and roast a whole hog.

The fat guy's love life is inextricably linked to his love of food. For the fat guy, food and sex are two points on a continuum. No fat guy would ever dream of making a move on a girl without first feeding her a nice meal—it's just not done. And when you're out with a fat guy you don't have to worry about looking like a pig. You can eat whatever you want, because nothing makes a fat guy hornier than a girl who can devour a big steak (although fat guys also appreciate skinny girls because they represent leftovers). As an aside, fat guys can hold their liquor. This is a simple biological fact. Remember those charts they show you in driver's ed? How much you can drink is a direct function of how much you weigh.

And who better to bring home to Mom than a fat guy? Mothers, especially immigrant mothers who speak little English and have yet to be co-opted by American neuroses, love men who can eat. They (correctly) equate eating prowess with intellect and potential for success.

The fat guy wages a stealthy seduction. The woman sees the fat guy as a confidant. She thinks the relationship is platonic. Eventually, she marries the fat guy. Sound familiar?

When it comes to sexual prowess, women in the know prefer fat guys because fat guys are better in bed. The thin and the fit like to demonstrate their manliness by getting on top and banging away, but no fat guy in his right mind would do the equivalent of 100 push-ups when he has the opportunity to lie on his back. Plus, do you know what the odds are of a girl getting off in the missionary position? If I have to tell you, you're obviously not a fat guy. But do you know what the odds are of a girl getting off when she's on top? Pretty damn good. And with minimal effort (i.e., reach down and help out with your fingers), you can make that a virtual lock (if that doesn't work, it's her problem—not yours). For every hard-bodied two-pump-chump out there, there's a fat guy ready to lie back and provide an erect instrument for as long as need be.

Fat guys are particularly well-suited to being passive sex partners for fit-and-trim athletic girls who have the stamina to ride all night. You've seen the couples; now you know why. If you want a man who will make the earth move, a fat guy is still your best candidate (see inertia and New-tonian physics, above). Remember when Chris Farley and Patrick Swayze had a dancing contest on *Saturday Night Live*? Yeah, you know what I'm talking about.

The best thing is that fat guys sincerely appreciate women who deign to sleep with them, because every fat guy harbors the deep-seated fear that he's unattractive. And really, what many women want (more so even than great sex) is to be appreciated. Fat guys are particularly apprecia-tive of fellatio, because it's the ultimate in minimum-effort sex, even less strenuous than masturbation. And fat guys are themselves masters of oral sex, because their mouths are so agile and in such good shape from all that eating (and because all they think about is sex, food, and maybe Seven of Nine on *Star Trek: Voyager*).

There was a time in history when, to get respect, you had to be fat. It meant you were affluent. It meant you were healthy. Now it's all twisted around: You can never be too thin or too rich, they say. But while it's possible nowadays for anybody on food stamps to maintain an impressive body weight by eating potato chips and Entenmann's chocolate doughnuts, the fat-as-healthy stereotype is making a comeback—at least in the gay community—and it's only a matter of time before straight people catch on.

It's simple: As my friend David, the gaiest guy I know, put it to me, "Everybody knows fat guys don't have AIDS. In the gay community, fat is in."

I pity the thin. They spend their lives fighting the inevitable weight gains that come with age, butting heads with their chubby destinies. When they finally get fat, which they all do, they become inconsolable. Their spouses and partners, terrified by this harbinger of what is to come for them, are likely to up and leave. The formerly thin die miserable and alone, raging against the injustice that has befallen them.

The lifelong fat guy experiences no such problems. He's a rock, a source of stability for all around him. He was fat as a child and remains fat. He looks no worse in middle age than at age twenty, and therefore his lifetime of fatness keeps him looking young (plus, it is well-known in the dermatological community that fat equals fewer wrinkles).

I was a fat kid, and I took some flak for it. But now, as I enter my thirties, all my formerly svelte friends are getting fat—and I'm having the last laugh. As my long-lost friend Andy said to me ten years after we graduated from high school, "You guys who were fat in high school are the only happy people at the high school reunion—we've all gotten fatter; you look the same."

Now, I'm enjoying my life, whereas my slowly ballooning friends are consumed by the battle against fat. They climb pretend stairs, "spin" on pretend bicycles, and run for dear life on treadmills. They deprive themselves of bodily pleasure, engage in self-indulgent and self-righteous fad dieting (no meat one month; no carbohydrates the next) and are otherwise miserable companions. They are particularly insufferable at the dinner table, because they are driven by an irresistible impulse to deliver a running commentary on the nutritional and medical ramifications of every bite they (and I) eat.

Yet, self-righteous though they may be, the joke's on them. Thinness is an unattainable goal. We've all seen the charts and tables—you know, the ones that say the "ideal weight" for a 5-foot-7 man is 138 pounds. Maybe that's what people weigh in television fantasyland, but, according to Kathryn Putnam Yarborough, a therapist at the Center for Eating Disorders at St. Joseph Medical Center in Towson, Maryland, "Less than 5 percent of the population, healthfully and genetically, can expect to achieve the shapes and sizes the media portrays as ideal. The media holds this unrealistic goal up to us and suggests that we try to reach it. No wonder so many men and women are struggling with body-image dissatisfaction."

I have a seemingly convincing excuse for being fat: I'm a restaurant reviewer. I'm supposed to be fat. But being fat requires no excuses and, truth be told, most restaurant reviewers are skinny—which perhaps accounts in part for the current sorry state of the food press. Never trust a skinny chef, even less a skinny restaurant reviewer. Would you believe it has now become commonplace for restaurant reviewers to negotiate gym memberships as part of their employment agreements? It's a latter-day myth of Sisyphus.

Speaking of myths, Western culture's belief that thin is better is a rejection not only of common sense but also of basic human instinct. Children and animals (the most anthropologically pure subjects available) love fat guys. Watch the baby's face light up when it sees a fat guy. Watch the dog beg for a fat guy's attention. They understand.

Non-Western cultures, which invariably have less emotional baggage than ours, revere fat guys. The fat Buddha is worshipped the world over. Only in self-flagellatory

Western religions are our idols so anorexic. Look how skinny Jesus was. Look what happened to him.

But, you say, being fat is unhealthy.

The thin see this as the trump card in any discussion of weight. But even if the statistics are true, even if being fat is unhealthy, can we really do anything about it? Despite the $33 billion a year that Americans spend on weight-loss programs, the Federal Trade Commission reports that 95 percent of the 50 million Americans who will go on diets this year will fail. Even better, according to the Center for Eating Disorders, "33–50 percent of these people gain to a higher weight," which means we're talking about a serious waste of money.

Although near-constant attention is paid to the health risks of being fat (the National Institutes of Health says that "someone who is 40 percent overweight is twice as likely to die prematurely as an average-weight person," and the American Heart Association calls obesity a "major risk factor" in heart disease), the consequences of the war on fat are largely ignored. Yet the unquestionable harms of eating disorders and diet-drug abuse surely must be weighed against the largely speculative harms attributable to weighing more than the "ideal" weight. For example, the Center for Eating Disorders' records indicate that eight million Americans suffer from anorexia, bulimia, and various other disorders—and 20 percent of these people experience premature death.

Moreover, the one statistic glaringly missing from most mortality studies is quality of life. How much happier is the person who lives life free of the constant pressure of negative body-image and fad dieting? How many days, months, or even years of life is that happiness worth?

Still, perhaps there is another explanation for the statistics.

Have you considered that the so-called evidence on weight and mortality has been fabricated? That a secret brotherhood of fat guys has engineered what can only be described as the most effective disinformation campaign in human history? That fat guys want to keep you thin, miserable, afraid, and powerless so they can enjoy the fruits of your labor?

Think about it. Fat guys sit around and eat whatever they want. Meanwhile, they tamper with the statistics and use fear of obesity to sap the thin of their energy and will. They keep the thin exercising and distracted, like rats in a maze, like gerbils on a Habitrail.

This master plan also includes a carefully cultivated image that allows fat guys to manipulate the thin into doing their work. The fat guy sits behind a desk all day, most likely screwing his secretary, while the secretary's athletic husband is out fighting fires (fat guys have made it very difficult for themselves to pass the firefighters test), protecting democracy (fat guys have arranged it so that the military will not accept overweight recruits), or otherwise creating wealth for fat guys to exploit. The fat guy holds the ladder while the thin ascend, risking life and limb to do the fat guy's bidding.

Actors are thin; producers are fat. Candidates are thin; chiefs of staff are fat. The fat guy retreats from the spotlight, content to be served. Content to rule the world.

And so, the next time you see a fat guy eating a double cheeseburger or struggling up a flight of stairs, do not pity him. Be afraid. Be very afraid.

Big Game Hunters

It started with Rick's dad, who was never a big presence in his life. His mother raised him; his dad, Rick says dismissively, was your typical West Side Cleveland drunk. But he could talk. And he liked to talk about "sweat-hogging." A college friend, a good-looking guy, had been into it. "Let's go out and pick up some pigs tonight," the guy would say. He homed in on fat girls, demanded oral sex, then kicked them out of the car when he was done. "He'd literally boot 'em out with his foot," Rick says, telling the story just as his dad told it to him.

When Rick and his friends headed out for the night, his dad would inevitably ask, "You guys going sweat-hogging?"

In high school, Rick lost his virginity to a large woman. It only escalated from there. He eventually dropped the "sweat." But hogging—that was something he got good at. Good at doing, good at talking about, just like his dad.

Rick is sitting at the Treehouse patio, a bar in Cleveland, drinking bottles of Bud with his roommate Mark and telling me about hogging. Rick is tall, broad, twenty-three, a salesman who looks like a construction worker. Mark is three years older, shorter, with a shy grin that women love. At first, both are hesitant to discuss the subject. Hogging, after all, is something men talk about with men, not women, and certainly not a woman taking notes. But they can't help themselves. After just one beer, they're egging each other on, jockeying for time, trying to top each story with something bigger and better.

Rick explains the attraction bluntly: "It's not something you aspire to, but no one decent is going to talk to you when you're at the bar with your friends, doing shots of Jäger. Sometimes you just say, 'Fuck it, let's get a pig.'"

It's not that they prefer fat women, they say. It's just easier.

"You're not embarrassed getting shot down by them," Mark says. "You're not embarrassed when they leave."

Mark's had nothing but big women for a long time. On a woman of average height, he'll go up to 160, 170 pounds—225 if it's St. Patrick's Day or New Year's Eve.

"I wake up and see monsters in his bed," Rick says, feigning horror.

Mark doesn't dispute their size. But he resists the "monster" label. He feels sorry for them, sorry for using them, sorry for being a jerk. If his friends don't find out, he'll call them. Do it again. "The problem is, sometimes they're really nice people."

These guys learned the rules of the game early: Slender women were the ones to get. If they were going to go after fat ones—or, horror of horrors, if they actually preferred them—they damn well better have something crass to say about it.

Just by acknowledging a certain softness, Mark is treading on dangerous ground.

Rick will have none of it.

"I just talk to them like they're complete disgusting pigs," he says. "You gotta break 'em down with insults. Comment on their fat—'You're a dirty little pig.' They call me a dick, an asshole, but after a few beers, they're into it."

"He's good because he has no conscience," Mark says mournfully.

I'd never heard of "hogging" until a guy friend, a sensitive writerly type, got an unsolicited tutorial from two coworkers. He couldn't believe they were serious. And I couldn't believe the responses I got when I started asking around. Too many guys seemed to know exactly what I was talking about; their only concern was that a woman was doing the asking. "You're not supposed to know about that!" one guy, a lawyer, exclaimed. Just by saying the word I had infiltrated the fraternity.

But once the word was out there, it wasn't hard to egg them on. In hogging, much of the fun seems to come in the telling, in recounting the tale that can top all others. Part of the appeal for guys like Rick is envisioning the graphic story they can tell their buddies later. "He loves it," explains his roommate, Mark, "and he loves telling the story."

For certain men—typically guys in their twenties and thirties, boozers all—hogging tales are like their grandfathers' fishing stories: oft-repeated and always embellished. There's the one that got away. The one who capsized the boat. The biggest whale of all.

As long as their real names aren't used, most hoggers eagerly detail their greatest hits—insisting at the top of their lungs just how off-putting they found the act. It's something to do when they are desperate, they claim. Or it's a prank, something gross to endure so as to later regale their friends.

A true enthusiast, Rick runs through his Rolodex of hogging adventures with little prompting. There was the secretary, with her big white breasts. "She was a perfect hog." Beautiful face, big soft body. His ex-girlfriend's sister: "She was a little porker, and I violated her every way."

Rick tells me about the girl who gave him and a friend oral sex in the front seat of a Ford Explorer. His friend wanted to take it further, but Rick dissuaded him: "Most of the time, you're not going to bang 'em," he explains, disgusted by the thought. Rick doesn't really prefer fat women, he insists; what gets him off is "violating" them. But while few hoggers take such obvious delight in degrading women, their protestations serve the same purpose. They were drunk. Or desperate. Or both.

"Take home a big girl, and the next day, you say you went hogging," says Jake, a thirty-five-year-old bartender. "It's not like it's the plan. It's the backup plan."

Jake did his hogging right after he'd broken up with his girlfriend. "The next day I was, like, how did this happen? Well, it just happens."

Scott, a thirty-year-old from Broadview Heights, met an obese woman at Knucklehead's in Parma on St. Patrick's Day. He'd been drinking since 8 A.M. They made out at the bar, then he took her home. The next morning, he made up an excuse to get her to leave; he actually circled the block in his car until she left. But when he ran into her two weeks later, they did it again. His friends gave him a hard time: "You went home with a hog."

His ready answer: "I got laid. What's your point?"

On a slow night at the bar, hogging becomes a group activity. Chris and his friends use a strategy they call "the scud missile." Confronted with a group of hot girls and one heavy, they designate their drunkest comrade as the missile. "We'll say, 'It's 11 o'clock, we're going to launch him!' " The drunk is deployed to woo the big girl; the rest of the posse follows five minutes later and moves in on her friends.

Sometimes the drunk closes the deal; sometimes he doesn't. His friends are always grateful. "Hey, we scored, too," Chris says. "We don't say nothin'." Some guys claim that hogging is a "slump-buster": Sex with a fat woman, they say, can break a string of bad luck and lift morale. (As former Arizona Diamondbacks first baseman Mark Grace once explained, even pro athletes have been known to do it.) It can also be an act of selflessness: A guy "jumps on the grenade" by taking the fat friend, clearing his pal's way to the skinny one.

The common denominator is extreme emotional detachment. Scott tells me about a friend who slept with a hog. Scott called the next day to taunt him. "You didn't cuddle with her in the morning, did you?"

He repeats his friend's answer with glee: "No, I stepped over her fat ass and left!"

Mark and his friend Alex take me to the Fox & Hound in Parma, a city Mark considers hog heaven. They want to show me how it's done.

Mark is nervous about the evening. He doesn't always score, he explains. If he strikes out, I'll have to cut him some slack. He's a loser around women. Plus, there may not be any hogs out.

Alex rolls his eyes. The hogs are always out, he says.

Sure enough, Mark manages to find one while he's

buying the first round. She might as well have EAGER tattooed on her back. She's poured into a red halter top, faux leather pants that lace up the side, and chunky stacked-heel boots.

They banter, and Mark buys her a shot. He returns to the table, excited. "She's perfect," he says. "A perfect little pig."

"Ask her to join us," Alex suggests.

"I did," Mark says. "But she's waiting for her food. How novel."

A few minutes later she sidles past the table, then slips and wipes out. "Another shot!" Mark calls.

"You're supposed to catch me," she says, giving a sidelong glance as she heads toward the bathroom.

"This is going to be great," Mark hisses. "I might get a blow job out of this. Right here in the parking lot."

"If you wake up with that the next morning..." Alex warns.

"I've done worse," Mark says blithely.

Leather Pants invites the guys to ladies' night at a bar called Quotes. We follow. The place is packed—with men.

Then darkness falls: Leather Pants is with another guy. A big guy. She accepts a light for her cigarette, but that's about it.

"You can't just go out with the mind-set that you're going to get a hog," Mark explains. "You can't."

We end up at a cop bar called Dina's, drinking Budweisers and talking about hogging. Mark sheds no tears for the hog who got away. "I think she might have been strung out on crack anyway," he says. "Did you see how her hand was shaking?"

Still, he wonders about his own track record: "When's the last time you've seen me with a hot chick?" Mark demands, then answers his own question: "You probably haven't."

To be sexy, you're supposed to be skinny. Kate Moss is just the extreme version of the broader truth: You don't see women bigger than a size 6 on a magazine cover. Or playing love scenes in the movies.

And so, when it comes to sex, fat women are the punch line. From Parma to Mentor, two towns close to Cleveland, the themes are the same. So are the jokes. "Fat women are like mopeds," they'll say. "They're fun to ride, but you wouldn't want your friends to see you."

"Slap her thighs and ride the wave in."

"Roll her in flour and find the wet spot."

Stories deriding fat women are everywhere. Jamie, who grew up on the East Coast, first heard of hogging at the University of Michigan. He uses "coyote arm" to convey the horror: "You'd chew off your own arm in the morning to get out of there without waking her up."

One grad student tells me that a friend participated in a hogging ritual at the U.S. Naval Academy. Sailors going on leave would throw money into a pot; the one who displayed the biggest pair of panties the next morning took all. But when the guy who supposedly participated surfaces, he says he wasn't actually involved: A friend had told him the story about his friends.

Another guy, an architect, tells of some bored college kids from Medina who drew straws; the loser had to pick up a fat woman and bring her home. The two then had sex while his pals watched from the closet. (In hogging parlance, this is known as "logging closet time.") "He knew his friends were watching, so the guy would be like, 'Call me Mr. President,'" the architect explains. "She did it, too."

But when he finds the Medina man who told the story, it wasn't his crew after all. It was one of his friend's friends; no one can tell me who or where they are today. Like all urban legends, the boldest stories always happened to someone else. Naturally, the more savage the act, the better the chance that the guy telling the story didn't do it—his buddy did. And the buddy, just as frequently, is impossible to track down.

With stories like that in constant circulation, it would be hard for any man to admit he's into zaftig women. Bryan, twenty-nine, tells me about meeting a fat woman at karaoke night. One minute she was applauding his performance, the next they were singing a duet. Soon they were making music of their own in the parking lot.

He enjoyed it, he says. But he's not about to follow up the way he might if she were thinner. "I might see her again, I might not," he says, adding, "If I do, I hope none of my friends are there."

Even Rick, for all his bravado, won't talk about his exploits with just anyone. He has a foolproof way of sussing out his audience: He'll wait for a fat woman to walk by, then make a comment about how he'd like to "stick it to her."

His companion's reaction is everything, Rick explains. "If he's disgusted, I'll say, 'Oh, I'm just kidding.' If he's like, 'Oh yeah, I'd do that,' you know he's with you. He's not afraid."

In college, Scott's friends used to declare "No Pride Night" whenever they hit a dry spell. The call of the evening: "Let's just go find anything."

They made sure to emphasize that it was an act of desperation—and only an act of desperation. If that meant turning it into a joke, so be it. "In college especially, you're just too lazy for a good-looking girl," Scott says. "So you find the ugliest, most disgusting one you can find and take her home. Then it's a joke. And if your friends give you a hard time, you say, 'I got a blow job. What about you?'"

Sometimes, the joke went beyond a joke. It became elaborate, and vicious. Growing up in Bay Village, Chris and his football pals only joked about hogging. In a town where most of the girls were pretty, there wasn't much more to do than talk.

Then he went away to college in Minnesota. There was a tight group of fourteen guys on his floor, and the ones returning for their sophomore year explained the drill to the freshmen: They'd each donate $100. Then they'd go barhopping. If one of the guys found a willing hog, everyone would hurry back to the dorm to surreptitiously watch the guy usher his prize into the room—and neglect to lock the door behind him.

The pack of thirteen would wait outside.

With cameras.

Inside, Chris says, the guy would mount his woman doggy-style. "We'd be outside the door…And he'd yell, 'Hi-ho-rodeo!'" Chris pauses for dramatic emphasis.

"And then we'd all run in and take a picture."

At the end of the year, the guy who'd rodeoed the biggest girl collected the pot, all $1,400 of it.

Competition was fierce. "Eight of us did it," Chris says. One guy did it three times. "Mine was 250, 260 pounds. And I didn't win. The guy that won it, she was large. Probably 280, 290.

"It was very hard, because you're not attracted to them," Chris adds, laughing. "It was difficult, because you get her clothes off, you see the side rolls. It just turns you off. You gotta suck yourself up and just do it. You got to."

Even after listening to guys talk about this stuff for weeks, the story is shocking. Chris sees that I'm perturbed. He blushes, but he doesn't get defensive: "It was one of my college classics." His friends, he says, all think it's funny.

"Yeah, it's bad, but you're not thinking about that. You're thinking it's hilarious—and it is."

The hoggers I meet are unfailingly polite. They arrive on time, offer to buy me drinks, stand when I get up to use the bathroom. When I mention I've recently gotten divorced, they are sympathetic. At the end of the night, they walk me to my car and wait to make sure it starts.

Their prey gets treated differently. I am thin; they have a different standard for women who are plus-sized. "Fat chicks need lovin', too," is often the closest they come to acknowledging their needs.

Many guys claim the hog should be, and often is, grateful for their attentions. "Fat chicks never get laid, because no one wants to see 'em naked," Scott explains.

"They feel appreciative just because a guy will let them give him a blow job," adds his friend Justin.

"They understand their place," Rick says. "They know they're pigs. They don't get it like a normal girl could. They're desperate."

Women aren't exactly clamoring to tell their side of the story. Some may be oblivious to the way they're being discussed; "hogging" is a term few women have even heard. Others, like the women at Chris's college, may be too embarrassed to tell even their closest friends. No woman wants to think of herself as a hog, much less let her girlfriends see her that way. The victims are silent.

And many hoggers admit to having few female friends. They see women as alien creatures whose motives are suspect. It's only a small leap to rationalize their piggish behavior by insisting that women are just as bad.

The excuses are many: Women are all hunting for a sugar daddy anyway. They mock men for their small size or limited stamina. In a hogger's way of thinking, it's only right that men return the insult. "You've got the other end of the coin, too," explains Mike, who owns a Lakewood bar. " 'He only lasted thirty seconds!' Stuff like that."

Some guys even admit they go for hogs because it's the only door open to them. "Sure, we could hit on good-looking chicks, but we're such West Park retards, it doesn't happen," Rick says.

"We've lowered our standards so low, they're no standards at all," Mark adds. But Mark admits that he sees fat women differently than some of his friends. He claims to be genuinely "remorseful" about his behavior; he gets bummed out sometimes just talking about it.

When he dates the occasional thin woman, he'll flaunt her around town and introduce her to his friends. But it's the fat ones he really likes. "They don't expect anything," he says, a bit defensively, then sighs. "They're just cool."

Rick Gilmour, a WTAM radio shock jock out of Cleveland, prides himself on being a misogynist—or at least a man who can appeal to misogynists and their prized eighteen-to-thirty-six-year-old demographic. In person, he's more gangly than his radio voice would suggest; he looks like the guy who ran the school audiovisual department, not the one who partied with the rugby team.

He's been known to refer to "hogging" on the air. He just assumes that his listeners know what he's talking about. His usual fare is politics or music or cars. Disparagement of fat women fits right into the mix; never mind that his own feelings are actually a bit more complex.

One of Gilmour's regular haunts, Backdraft's, is a hole-in-the-wall tucked into a Lorain Road strip mall. Gilmour knows most of the guys here; the only woman is a tired fortysomething giving full attention to her drink. "You'd never know it from this sausage fest," he says, "but this is Ladies' Night."

I've told Gilmour I want to talk about hogging, so he comes suitably prepared with a steady patter of hogging jokes. He tries the roll-her-in-flour line. I can't help it. I groan. "There are no new jokes, just people to hear them," he says, a little defensively.

A mustachioed Army vet on the next barstool lights up a smoke. "Hey, you know what they say: more cushion for the pushin'."

"Any port will do in a storm," Gilmour agrees.

The Mustache leans in. At Ohio State in the '60s, he says, he went to something called a Green Dot party. "Whoever brought the ugliest girl got the prize," he says.

What did the women think? I ask.

"Who cared?" says The Mustache.

Gilmour admits he's been with some heavies. He professes not to like it. "In polite society, they call 'em Rubenesque. Some people say it's softer, it feels better." Not him: "I'll take a chance with a woman where our hip bones are knocking together." The Mustache laughs.

Gilmour's friend Bryan sidles over. At twenty-nine, he's got a house in the burbs and one of those job titles—tech-support specialist—that could mean he's anything from a software programmer to a janitor.

Gilmour explains the topic, and Bryan sips his MGD thoughtfully. "It's a situation where you could either play golf with a high handicap or a low one," he says philosophically. "Sometimes you just feel like winning the game."

When it gets to be 12:30, there are only two hours left in the evening, "unless you count Denny's, which I don't," Bryan explains. So he takes what he can. "Fat chicks may be just as lonely and bored as you are."

Last time he did it: a month ago. Worst time: a 220-pounder, sister of his pal.

Fortunately, he was at a friend's college campus at the time, not his own. "This was the perfect situation," he says. "I was in Toledo; I knew one person."

But, Bryan adds, he would have done it even if his entire college had been there. "The fallout just would have been greater," he says.

Or he could lie, I suggest. Claim he didn't really do it.

"You don't lie about it," Bryan says, horrified.

"You just say, 'Fat chicks need loving, too,' " Gilmour says.

Bryan takes a long swig. Then he makes a confession. "Really, I think the prettiest women look like Marilyn Monroe, Bettie Page. They had meat on their bones."

"Jayne Mansfield," Gilmour agrees, in almost a reverie. "We're talking real meat."

One of my good friends in college was overweight. She was pretty—red hair, beautiful blue eyes, flawless skin. But the guys I tried to set her up with were instantly and firmly opposed. To one guy, my suggestion even triggered a personal crisis. "Is that what you think of me? You think that's the best I can do?"

Guys aren't supposed to be with fat women. A girl can have buckteeth, bad acne, or a flat chest. It's excusable; fat isn't.

And that's where "hogging" comes from. For certain guys, if you've been with a plus-sized woman, you don't just need ironic distance: You need to summon up the proper amount of horror. So there are the self-deprecating jokes: I'm just a dumb drunk; I've gotta get laid, don't I? The stories they share with their tribe often mask a certain defensiveness: She was huge; this was more a gross-out *Jackass*-style stunt than anything related to love. Or, what I really got off on was degrading her.

Some of these guys actually prefer heavier women. But

they can hardly admit it, even to themselves. It's too alien to the way their friends talk.

And so there's a constant thread: It's only hogging. I didn't really like her. I want what I'm supposed to want, a slender woman, and preferably one with large breasts.

Back at the Treehouse, night is falling, and the conversation is growing windy. "Perfect hogging is big fat tits, fat thighs, but a good-looking face," Rick explains.

"The hogs don't think they're hogs, ever," Mark says.

Rick is getting philosophical. "It's not the way my mom said I should be to women, but it works. I don't make the rules, I just play the game."

When the time comes, Rick says, he'll pass down the rule book, just like his dad did to him. "When my kid's in college, sure I'll say something," Rick says. "Of course."

"If he was going to homecoming with a big cow, I'd say it to my wife: 'He likes hogging,' " Mark says. "But not to him."

"I wouldn't tell my wife," Rick says. "Some things you keep to yourself."

Mark doesn't buy it. "He can't keep it in," he taunts.

"They are great stories," Rick protests, "but to tell your dudes!"

The patio is pitch-black by the time Andy and Ben join our group. Both Mark and Rick are thrilled: Ben, they explain, is the perfect guy to talk about hogging. He always has a heavy woman on his arm. He dates 'em. He revels in 'em.

But Andy quickly sets us straight. Ben, he says, doesn't hog. "But he likes hogs." Ben explains that he likes a woman with a big butt, a firm fat shape. "I don't care how big it is, as long as it's firm. I think even you would be shocked at how big you can get and still be firm," he tells Rick.

"But she's still a hog to me," Mark protests.

Ben doesn't agree. "I know what I like. These guys find something I like to be a joke. They like to laugh about it and retell it. But they may find it gives them some reserve of pleasure. They're expanding their definitions of what is attractive."

Rick has grown quiet.

When he finally speaks, he is struggling with new thoughts. I can see the wheels turning.

"In a certain sense, he has a point," he says. "It's fat women I usually masturbate to. Because they get me off… I can't get Tyra Banks, nor do I want to. But there's something about violating this little pig that makes me happy." It's almost an epiphany. Still, the moment of reflection can only last so long. Within a minute, he and Mark are back to talking about how fat women give better oral, how they're disposable, how the hookup is fun because the woman is willing to be degraded.

Most important: It's a hookup and only a hookup. Never a girlfriend. Never wife material. "If it's a fat bitch, I don't want to see her afterward," Rick says.

"You're hogging," Andy says.

"I'm hogging," Rick agrees. "You don't want to have a hot bitch blow you off because she can. You want a fat bitch who'll suck your cock. Last call, I like to get my dick sucked rather than play euchre all night."

Rick takes a long swig of his beer. "That's the bottom line," he explains to the darkness. "That's hogging."

Fat Like Him

He didn't write like a fat guy. He didn't even have a fat guy's name. His name was Tim—concise, no silent vowels taking up extra space, two muscular consonants on each end. *Tiny Tim. Slim Tim.* In elementary school, the thin kids always had compact names like Dan or Ben or Ed. Except for Bob—with the round *o* and the blubbery *b*'s— whom we used to call "Blob." And Pat, who became known as "Fat." Tim, though—that was a solid name, a thin person's name.

"Column" read the subject line of Tim's first e-mail. I was, at the time, a singles columnist for a trendy magazine, and I'd get the occasional fan mail or stalker. But this note was different. It was irreverent, intellectual, and charming without being smarmy. After I published my memoir about teenage anorexia, I became an expert on what kind of person was writing. Or at least, what shape. Fat-person writing tended to be inappropriately revealing, needy, attention-seeking—emphasizing words or even entire phrases with oversized ALL CAPS, weighed down by protracted clauses connected by redundant ellipses, always wanting more, never being able to stop with a simple period.

Tim's writing was thin. It was sparse, nimble—the turns of phrases almost athletic in their deftness. Most notably, Tim didn't seem hungry like the fat folks: for advice, a correspondence, a date. His e-mail ended with the neutral, "Good luck."

Intrigued, I e-mailed back: "Who are you?" Minutes later, a reply arrived in my mailbox: "Me." His subject lines were always spare, like the title of a haiku. It turned out Tim was a twenty-eight-year-old associate at one of L.A.'s most prestigious law firms. Like me, he'd gone to an East Coast college, written for its paper, and competed in chess competitions. He signed off with his characteristic, "Good luck."

I went to his firm's Web site, expecting to find an overworked attorney with sunken cheekbones and dark circles under his eyes. But next to Tim's bio there was only an empty square, a placeholder for his photo. A Google search turned up some text but no pictures. There was a snippet about Tim finishing first in his law school class, and a blurb about him editing his college's humor magazine. A witty intellectual—exactly my type.

Over the next two weeks, we e-mailed several times a

day. Actually, I e-mailed and he responded with pithy messages peppered with bits of information: He'd been married for a year to an actress who was Julia Roberts' stand-in. His parents were academics. His younger brother was a comedy writer. I figured the brother got his sense of humor from Tim.

"No," Tim replied when I asked about his divorce. "I don't have any scars from the quickie marriage. Except for those extra 150 pounds."

"And I've got no scars from my recent breakup," I shot back. "My one-eyed thing, that happened at birth."

Despite the onslaught of flirtatious e-mails, Tim never asked to meet me, never acknowledged the romantic nature of our burgeoning relationship. I felt like I was chasing him: If I didn't e-mail, he wouldn't initiate one on his own. It seemed strange, given that we even had pet names for each other. I called him "Ralph" from his childhood obsession with *The Honeymooners;* he called me "Alice" in return.

"So, Ralph, are we ever gonna talk on the phone?" I wrote late one night. "My arms have cramps from all the typing." He once mentioned that he worked out at the gym in his building and I fantasized about his buff biceps. But when he didn't respond, I wondered if he'd told me the truth—was he still married? Did he have a girlfriend? Was he gay?

"Alice to Ralph," I wrote the next morning. "Do you have laryngitis?"

At midday, I sent one final missive.

"If I don't hear from you in thirty minutes, I'll assume *The Honeymooners* is over."

A minute later, Tim's trademark haiku appeared on my screen: "Number."

Tim didn't sound the way he wrote. His voice seemed to be trapped under a large rock. I thought I heard static, or heavy breathing.

"Are you on a speaker phone?" I said.

"Why?" Tim asked. "Are you?" Throughout our conversation, he often answered a question with a question. I couldn't tell if he was being cryptic or Talmudic.

"Does it feel weird to talk to me after all those e-mails?" I asked.

"Does it feel weird to you?" he replied.

"Are you close with your brother?" I asked.

"Are you close with yours?"

"Do you want to meet?" I tried.

"Do you?"

I was relieved when Tim suggested a romantic Italian restaurant midway between our apartments. I asked how we'd recognize each other.

"I've got black curly hair, and big brown eyes—some

might call them 'bedroom eyes,' " Tim quipped. "I'm 5'10″ and, like I said, I'm 150 pounds overweight."

"Okay," I laughed. "And I'll be the Cyclops with the pierced nose."

"I'm serious," Tim said.

"So am I," I deadpanned. "Do you know how hard it is to find a monocle with the lens fixed in the middle?"

After we hung up, Tim sent me an e-mail: "Truth." He insisted he wasn't kidding about his weight. I thought it was strange to play the joke this long, but then again, Tim was a bit of an eccentric. One night when he didn't respond to my e-mails, he explained he'd gotten stuck after-hours in the office elevator, and instead of pressing the emergency button, he decided to sleep there overnight "just for kicks." I liked that about him. I thought he was taking the schtick too far, but at least he had a sense of humor.

"Look for a fat guy, or you'll end up at the wrong table," Tim wrote.

"Then wear a flower in your lapel so I'll know it's you," I typed back.

What kidders we were.

The restaurant was dark, lit entirely by candles. It was his stomach I saw first—before the black curly hair and the brown bedroom eyes, before the red rose in his lapel. It was like this attractive guy had sextuplets in his belly. I averted my gaze, the way you're supposed to avoid staring at a veteran's stubby limb or a cancer patient's bald head. I wondered if it was too late to flee.

"Hey, you're not a Cyclops," Tim said, handing me the rose.

"I was just, you know…I'm sorry." Suddenly I felt self-conscious about my size, apologetic for being tiny and weighing less than 100 pounds.

"Well, at least *I* was honest." Tim smiled. He had beautiful teeth. How could teeth that labored to break down vast quantities of fatty food be in such good condition?

We didn't discuss Tim's weight. I'm not sure what we talked about. He seemed like a Charlie Brown character muttering "*WAH wah wah*" while I was busy examining his face. For a guy with that much blubber, his face looked pretty good. He wasn't the roly-poly kind of fat guy, the Chris Farley human sausage type. His eye sockets, cheeks, and lips looked almost normal, until you got to his jaw—the fleshy jowls. I watched them wobble up and down as he spoke.

"I'd like the house salad, no cheese, dressing on the side," he told the waiter.

"And for your entrée, sir?"

"Just the salad," Tim said. "I'm on a diet."

The waiter and I exchanged dubious glances. Tim pretended not to notice and I pretended not to notice him noticing.

I wanted to ask Tim about his diet, about how and why and when he'd gotten so fat, and whether he'd tried therapy or hypnosis or acupuncture or paid thousands of dollars to go on one of those fad diets advertised on billboards all over town. I wanted to know about practical things like cholesterol and fitting into movie theater seats and going to the bathroom and having sex. I wondered whether Tim had had sex since the breakup of his marriage two years before. I wondered what a fat guy's penis looked like and if, given his protruding belly, he could see it without looking in the mirror.

Instead I launched into a bumbling riff about my trip to the Washington Monument as a kid, and how I'd never seen anything like it in L.A., where we didn't have any monuments because people are such narcissists and all we have is the Hollywood Walk of Fame.

"I know what you're really thinking about," Tim interrupted when I got to the part about wanting to climb the stairs to the top of the monument.

"Yeah, what?"

"Whether I can see my penis."

I spat out some water, which mixed with the oily beads of perspiration on Tim's cheek.

"Don't be embarrassed," he said, wiping his face. "Everyone wonders. At least the women who're interested."

I tried to suppress my smile: *Women who're interested?*

"Look, Ralph," I said, softening my voice. I considered

taking his hand, but his fingers were so thick I didn't think mine would fit around them. "I like you a lot, I really do. It's just that meeting a total stranger is always a crapshoot. I mean, what are the odds there'll be chemistry in person?"

"You tell me. What are the odds?"

"I hope we can be friends," I said, looking away.

"Okay." He paused. "So you don't want to know if I can see it?"

"No," I laughed. "Well, yeah...but no."

"Aha!" Tim shouted, causing the fat on his neck to undulate like the earth's surface during a mild earthquake. "Too bad you'll never find out."

After dinner, waiting for our cars by the curb, we shook hands and mumbled awkward "nice to meet you's." The valet opened my car door.

"Good luck," Tim said, just like in his e-mails.

"Hey, Ralph," I called back. "Why do you always wish me good luck?"

"Because you'll need it to get over me," he smiled. Those teeth again. I wondered if he'd been a Colgate model when he was thin.

"Take care," I said, pulling away slowly to see what kind of car he'd fit into. They say people's dogs resemble their owners; did that apply to cars, too? I ran through a mental list of heavy-duty automobiles: a Volvo wagon, an Explorer SUV, a van like the ones serial killers use. Or maybe he'd gone the counterintuitive route with a sports car, or a compact two-door. I glanced at my side mirror. His car hadn't arrived yet, but I saw Tim by the curb—or most of him. His body was too wide for my mirror.

I pressed the accelerator, my eyes glued to the image of Tim's belly in the glass: MAN IN MIRROR IS LARGER THAN HE APPEARS.

"Well?" my friend Stella asked when I picked up the phone in the morning. "Was it great? Why didn't you call? He's not there with you, is he?"

"He weighs more than 300 pounds," I said. "He has no neck, he makes little wheezing noises just to breathe, and his butt actually jiggles." I'd seen his butt jiggle when he walked to the men's room.

"So he *was* serious!"

It seemed so idiotic now. After all of Tim's attempts to tell me about his weight, I'd refused to believe him. Partly because he was a joker, but mostly because he seemed so driven, ambitious, successful—he didn't fit the stereotype of the lazy fat guy who sits in front of ESPN eight hours each night stuffing his face with Doritos and dip. It was like assuming the beautiful girl with the big tits in high school must be a slut and not the valedictorian.

"That's insane!" Stella said. "You had so much chemistry. It was like, you had that 'zing.'"

She was right. I'd had more chemistry with Tim than

I'd had with my last boyfriend, the one with the fabulous washboard abs.

"Oh, well," I sighed. "So much for gut instincts."

When Stella called back in the afternoon, I was still in bed.

"What's wrong?" she asked.

"Nothing," I said. "I just thought it might be Tim calling. I mean, if a guy who's three times my weight isn't interested, how undesirable must *I* be?"

I knew Stella would understand. She'd recently gone on a blind date with an attractive paraplegic. They'd met online, and when he told her about his "situation," she felt obligated to keep their date—what kind of person would cancel? They shared a three-hour dinner, and Stella, who always gets asked on second dates, never heard from him again. She spent $500 at the shrink before realizing he probably assumed *she* wasn't interested.

"He probably assumes *you're* not interested," Stella said, parroting her therapist. "You even told him you only want to be friends."

"Maybe I should call him," I said.

"Why? If you continue the friendship, it'll prevent you from pursuing relationships with, you know, *real* men. He'll be like a gay friend. Except fat."

She had a point. You couldn't have sex with either. One

wouldn't be able to get it up for you, and the other would simply crush you.

"I'm not calling," I said. "But what about e-mail? I miss our e-mails."

"Just don't," she repeated. "Besides, it's not fair to him. He may think you're interested. Men are like that. A 300-pound woman would never assume a hot young guy is interested, but a 300-pound man? They're clueless. It's for his own good."

"Okay. I won't call—for his sake."

"I mean it," Stella said.

"Don't worry," I assured her. "I'm not calling."

I hung up with Stella and logged onto my e-mail. Nothing from Tim. At dinner he'd told me that his electronic apartment key had fallen out of his wallet, and that if he couldn't reach his landlord late at night, he'd have to climb up the fire escape onto his balcony to retrieve the hidden spare key. He lived on the fifth floor. I wondered if he'd been able to contact his landlord, or if the fire escape had broken to pieces under his weight. Maybe he was in the hospital with a broken neck. I called Stella back.

"Shouldn't I at least call to see that he's okay?" I asked.

"Don't you think he'd find it insulting that you're worried he broke the fire escape with his blubber?"

"You're right, I won't call."

"If you do, it'll be a *huge* mistake. No pun intended."

I thought of Tim's huge belly and remembered a

nightmare I'd had early in the morning about a clan of fat people who detach their guts, which are revealed to be angry creatures that attack normal-sized people. The memory made me shudder.

An hour later, I checked my e-mail again, but didn't see Tim's address. I pictured Tim at work, clicking on his e-mail, seeing nothing from me, and feeling the same sense of disappointment. Or maybe he'd forgotten all about me. He probably had plenty of friends and didn't need to add me to the list. After all, aren't fat people known for their friendliness? In movies and in life, aren't they always the funny sidekick-buddy—popular because they're so affable and nonthreatening? Entertaining and observant, because they've had to develop their personalities to compensate for their appearance? Maybe he'd written me off as one too many thin friends to handle. Maybe he wouldn't even take my call.

I picked up the phone to call Stella, but dialed Tim's number instead. His secretary put me straight through.

I'd already arranged the chess pieces on the board when Tim arrived at my house that Monday after work. The night before, I'd reminded him on the phone that this wouldn't be a date.

"I hear you, 'just friends,'" Tim said through what I now knew wasn't a speakerphone. "It'll be a chess date."

"Not a date," I corrected him. "Or at least not a *date* date."

"I get it," Tim said. "Who ever heard of a chess *date* date? Has Garry Kasparov ever gotten any while playing chess?"

When I opened the door, Tim held up a bottle of wine ("Not a date—all top chess players need wine for inspiration," he quickly explained) and walked straight into my kitchen to open it. I figured he was nervous and wanted to get some alcohol into his system. Or maybe he wanted an excuse to check out my kitchen, to see what foods I kept on the counter, in the cabinets and the fridge. He wore a vintage cardigan sweater over an untucked oxford, which did nothing to hide his belly but managed to minimize his butt. Back at the dining table, he set out two glasses by the chessboard: wine for me, water for him.

"My diet," he smiled, toasting me with his Evian. "I'll have to be otherwise inspired."

We sparred for four hours, him moving a knight to attack my bishop, me moving my bishop to attack his queen, him moving his rook to threaten mine. Occasionally, our hands would touch accidentally, but we'd both pull them away as though we'd touched an electric current and mutter embarrassed "oh sorry's" and "excuse me's." Around 11:30, I noticed Tim sneaking up on my king as he chased me around the board. At midnight, he trapped me and uttered, "Checkmate."

"It's only because I plied you with wine," Tim said

graciously. I felt light-headed and giddy. The wine had made me tipsy. Or horny. I was consumed by an urge to kiss Tim, but I wasn't sure why. Was it the novelty? I'd never been with a guy who'd beat me at chess before. Then again, I'd never been with a guy who had so much blubber. Was it the chess or the fat? Or simply the wine? All three were present at once—scientifically speaking, it wasn't a controlled experiment.

"I can't believe I lost," I said, clearing off the board. As I got up, the room started spinning.

"If it makes you feel any better, you're the best game I've ever had. No offense, but I didn't think you'd be that good."

I gave Tim a sideways glance. He stood to leave and I saw his face up close again—the aquiline nose, the fleshy jowls.

"Seriously, Alice. You had me scrambling to the very end. Then you got tired, I guess."

"Not tired, Ralph. Distracted." He gave me a questioning look, all wrinkled forehead and puckered lips. I couldn't help myself, with those puckered lips inches from my face. I leaned in from the side, avoiding his belly, and planted a kiss on his mouth.

Tim's lips were fleshier than they looked. It was like kissing a down pillow. His lap was like a Duxiana mattress that conforms to the shape of your body. I felt wetness on

my torso and noticed that Tim was utterly soaked, as if
he'd been rained on without a coat, or gone swimming in
his clothes. I'd never seen a person sweat so much. I worried he might go into cardiac arrest.

"Are you sure this is safe?" I asked.

"I guess we'll have to see," he said, picking me up and
carrying me into the bedroom. He took one look at my
delicate wrought-iron bed frame and suggested we try the
floor.

"I broke my chair at work," he explained. "And that
was an Aeron."

Tim's body resembled the topography of a Thomas'
English muffin, all those nooks and crannies made of cellulite. I envied the way he could strip off his clothes as
if he had Brad Pitt's body—unashamed, unapologetic—
whereas I often left my shirt on during sex to hide my
A-cups.

"Mystery solved," he said with a flourish, as he
struggled to slide his humongous boxers to his ankles. He
looked down and I realized he was referring to his cock
and the fact that I could see it—and he couldn't. Tim must
have understood what it's like to have a vagina, a sexual or-
gan that you can't see directly, but your lover can. I half expected his penis to be encircled by sheaths of fat, to be
proportionally portly and stout like his 300-pound frame,
but it was long and hard and muscular-looking, like an action figure he'd hidden in the folds of his skin.

"Fat free," I thought, watching this man, the size of a

hippo, naked and unselfconscious, now dancing a silly jig with the lights on. Did the expression mean more than dietetic yogurt or salad dressing? Was fat a *freeing* force, a force that erases inhibition and insecurity? Would we all be happier heavy, but "fat free"?

Fifteen years earlier, in my anorexia days, I wouldn't so much as shake hands with a fat person for fear of contagion. Now I had a fat person *inside* me. A primal part of me wanted to vomit, and another part didn't want it to end. I closed my eyes and pictured my athletic ex-boyfriend, a cute guy I'd seen earlier that day in the Whole Foods produce section, even Ben Stiller, but I couldn't resist peeking at Tim. Or, rather, looking through him. I was fucking his innards instead of his outers, making love to his soul instead of his body. Had a man ever done that with me?

I ripped off my blouse, my bra, and let Tim lick my nipples.

"I want to see you in the light," Tim said, positioning my torso in front of the lamp. I posed proudly, as if I'd just won a wet T-shirt contest on *Girls Gone Wild*. After all, he couldn't be judging my body. His breasts were bigger than mine.

When we finished, Tim immediately fell asleep. The buzz from the wine, the chess, the blubber, and even the sex quickly wore off, and I became sleepy and panicked at once. I considered waking Tim from the floor, but I didn't think he'd fit in the bed with me. Or if he did, it might come crashing down.

I'd just dozed off when a honking noise startled me awake. It sounded like a truck horn right outside my house. Then I noticed Tim. On my floor was a sweaty, smelly, three-hundred-pound man, mouth open, slobbering onto my rug, emitting the most irritating squawking sound I'd ever heard. As I got out of bed to look for earplugs, he let loose a cloud of gas so noxious that I became temporarily paralyzed, as if I'd been sprayed with a can of Mace.

Stella was right. This had been a huge mistake.

I was glad when Tim didn't call the next day. The day after, I was mad. The third day I became inexplicably sad. When he e-mailed the fourth day—the subject line read, "Saturday"—I replied, "Yes." We spent the next seven nights together.

While Tim was consumed by his diet, I was the one who lacked self-control. I couldn't stay away from him. He was like a magnet that both repelled and attracted me at once. I liked the banter, the chess games, the discussions of articles from the *New Yorker*. I even liked giving him blowjobs—sprawled across the cushion of his belly, swallowing his fatty cum that tasted like cream. But that wasn't enough to explain such intense physical chemistry with a man whose appearance—out of bed—repulsed me.

Or did it? They say there's a fine line between love and hate, and I was right on the razor's edge. How could I be so ashamed of the person I craved more than anybody? Was I projecting my shame about my own body onto Tim? Or had I finally discovered my true "type"—fatties—the way some women discover that their true type is really other women? I used to go for lanky, fit, small-boned Jewish-looking intellectuals, but none of those relationships had worked out. I wondered if my true self was closer to Sir Mix-A-Lot in "Baby Got Back" and I'd start going to "fatty bars" to pick up obese men. I once read an article about women who love fat men and have "fatty parties" at hip hot spots each month. I imagined joining their mailing lists. But at the food court in the mall, I'd see heavy men waddle by after wolfing down greasy cheeseburgers and I'd practically gag at the thought of sleeping with them.

If I couldn't explain the attraction to myself, how could I explain it to my friends? I didn't even try. Tim was like a secret drug habit that led to a series of evasions, equivocations, and outright lies.

"I ran into that cute writer at Starbucks," Stella said after I'd screened out her last five calls. "He told me you blew him off for a date tonight. What are you doing?"

"I'm busy," I said. "You know, work."

"You don't have two hours to meet him for dinner? What are you working on?"

"It's not two hours," I said. "I'd have to blow-dry my hair, shave my legs, figure out what to wear, dig up some panties without holes, smell good." That was the beauty of Tim. I did none of that for him and he lusted after me anyway.

"I think you should go out with Josh," Stella said.

"Why?"

"Because you need to get laid. It's been, what, six months? You haven't slept with anyone since the breakup, have you?"

I laughed my best liar's laugh. "Of course not," I said. "Who would I have slept with?"

After we'd been sleeping together for a month, Tim had an announcement to make: "I want to take you out to dinner."

I wanted to join the Witness Protection Program.

Our routine had been to order delivery, have sex, and by the time we were done an hour later, the food would arrive. But Tim was on a strict diet—no sugar, no dairy, no oil—and the orders proved too confusing even for L.A. restaurants.

"Don't you think ordering in is more fun?" I said, but Tim had started going to Overeaters Anonymous meetings, and apparently, by not supporting his dietary needs, I was being an "enabler."

"Okay," I conceded, "we'll go out. But if you're really serious about losing weight, you have to finish eating before 6 P.M." I figured nobody would see us in restaurants if we left by 6.

Aside from our first meeting, I'd never been in public with Tim. I couldn't imagine being in public with Tim.

Heck, I couldn't imagine how Tim could be in public with Tim. Wasn't he ashamed of all that waddle? Didn't he cringe at the possibility of people looking at him and thinking, "Poor guy. And so young, too." And wouldn't they pity me as well? Wouldn't they wonder what's wrong with a girl who's so hard up for love that she has to date a guy who needs two napkins to cover his lap? *Poor girl. And so young, too.*

I came up with tricks to avoid being touched by Tim in public. I brought reading material to meals so I could keep one hand occupied by the book, the other by a utensil. I made sure to wear jackets with pockets and, on warm days, switched to pants with front pockets so I could bury my hands away from Tim's hungry paws. Once, while walking to Tim's car near the sushi place, we fell into a laughing fit and he grabbed my free hand. It took me a moment before I realized what had happened, and I jerked my arm away, as though I'd accidentally touched the flame on a stove.

"What's wrong?" Tim asked.

"Nothing," I lied, quickly reaching up to scratch my nose. "Allergies. There must be a lot of pollen in the air."

"I didn't know you had allergies," Tim said.

"Yep." I added a fake sneeze for good measure. Nobody wants to hold a snotty hand.

"Is that what you used to weigh?" I asked Tim one night when he told me his target was 180 pounds. To reach that, I realized, he'd have to lose my entire weight. I was 5'2" and 100 pounds. He was 5'10" and 280. Had he really gained an entire person since his divorce?

"I actually weighed 160, but I'm giving myself some leeway," he said.

"One-sixty! Is that even healthy?"

Tim shrugged. "Everyone in my family is naturally skinny." I tried not to look at his tree-trunk legs.

"Can I see pictures?" I asked.

"Why?"

"I'm just curious to see what you looked like."

He smiled mischievously. "But if I give you a preview, it'll be anticlimactic."

"Oh, come on," I persisted. "Let me see your driver's license!" I grabbed for Tim's wallet but he tossed it in the air and began juggling with it. He was a really good juggler. Quick and agile, like a thin person. "Patience, my dear, is a virtue," he teased as his wallet whizzed by.

Later that night, while he slept—he'd recently moved from the floor to my bed, where his body heat warmed me like a furnace—I sneaked across the room to peek in his wallet. He traveled light: two credit cards, a health insurance card, an auto club card, a key card, and a frequent buyer card from a lunch place called Healthy Eats. The plastic compartment reserved for a driver's license was empty. I wondered what his real motivation for hiding his photo was.

Maybe, I thought, he'd never been thin at all.

The more sex I had with Tim, the more hungry I became. Not just for his body, but for food. Sex with Tim was wild, uninhibited, and exhausting. Tim had been working out with a trainer, and his stamina improved dramatically. For a guy who became short of breath while merely sitting at his desk drafting high-level litigation, somehow he managed to make love to me twice some nights. His arms had become strong enough to hold his weight above me, so I no longer had to be on top. I began eating an extra meal at midnight—partly because we finished dinner so early, and partly to regain my strength.

Tim was losing more than five pounds a week, and I wondered what it would be like going to dinner with him when things were normal. There was something twisted about a tiny girl eating a plate of sausage fettuccine while her humongous dinner companion got the dry lettuce. Wherever we went, the waiter would serve me the diet plate and Tim the hamburger or chicken parmigiana. We'd say, "No, over there," but the waiter would still give me the salad and we'd have to switch the plates ourselves.

"You can't keep isolating yourself," Stella said on the phone one afternoon as Tim was on his way over. "Amy and I have been talking, and we think you're depressed. You never go out, you don't see anyone, you turn down every invitation that comes your way. It's not healthy."

"I'm going out tonight," I said.

"You are? With who?"

"A guy I met. But I don't want to talk about it yet." I'd been considering introducing Tim to my friends when he reached 230, but I got ahead of myself. I had a problem with premature revelation.

"Come on," Stella said. "Tell me *something* about him."

"Well," I hedged. "He's a lawyer. He's funny, he's smart, he's creative, and, I don't know, there's just this amazing connection."

"Tell me more!" Stella pleaded.

"Not yet."

"Hey," Stella said. "You know who he sounds like?"

"Who?"

"Remember that fat guy you met? He sounds like that fat guy, but thin."

"Exactly," I replied. "A thinner version of the fat guy." The Tim he was becoming. Or the Tim he used to be? I wasn't sure.

"I'll be right back," Tim said as parked in the garage beneath his apartment complex. We'd just gone to one of our "early-bird" dinners on Tim's side of town, and he needed to pick up a change of clothes before we went back to my place. I asked to come up.

"Okay," he said. "But it's nothing special. *She* got all the furniture, and I haven't done much to replace it."

While Tim went to retrieve a clean suit, I stood in the

empty space and looked around. It seemed like a tiny apartment for such a big guy, a dollhouse for a Doberman. Aside from the Berber carpets, fireplace, and modernist artwork, there wasn't a single piece of furniture in the entire place. No wonder Tim hadn't minded sleeping on my floor.

Only the kitchen showed signs of life: beautiful cookware, fancy appliances, fully stocked candy jars, and pasta canisters—gifts from a wedding gone awry. A large, glass rectangular sugar bowl, the size of a small aquarium, contained a single layer of particles on the bottom, and I wondered if the bowl had once been filled to the top and Tim inhaled the white powder like cocaine until he blew up to over 300 pounds.

The refrigerator was covered with lists: Tim's food diary, his daily weight chart, his OA meeting times. Next to the lists was an Einstein magnet pressing a photo to the door: Julia Roberts embracing a skinny guy in a tux. No, wait—Tim's ex-wife and the old Tim! The 160-pound Tim. So he'd been telling the truth after all. He'd lost a wife and gained her weight back in kind. In a weird way, he was carrying around a person who couldn't leave him—unless he so chose.

"Hey!" Tim said, grabbing the photo from me. He stood behind me, holding a hanging bag.

"You look great."

"Let's go." He slipped the photo into the drawer, slamming it shut. I'd never seen Tim angry before.

"I'm sorry."

"I wanted it to be a surprise."

"It was! I mean, you look so..."

"I must look hideous by comparison," he said.

"You don't," I lied. Tim looked amazing in the photo, sporting his fitted tux and flashing an insouciant smile. His gleaming teeth and chiseled cheekbones made my heart speed up. I tried to find this image in the guy standing before me, but it was like those cruise ship brochures where the spacious cabin in the photo turns out to be the size of a cat box. Here, though, the toned, lean frame in the photo turned out to be twice the size in person.

"I wish you hadn't seen it. I hate that photo."

"Well, maybe you could cut her out of it, or choose a photo of you alone at that weight. I'd imagine seeing yourself that thin is an incentive, right?"

"It's not an incentive," he said. "It's a cautionary tale."

I gave him a curious look, but he turned and walked out the door.

People gaped at me when we walked into Tim's Overeaters Anonymous meeting. I must have looked positively skeletal in that crowd of obese people sitting in a semi-circle and chatting like old friends.

The night before, Tim had told me he'd be "sharing" at

the meeting and asked me to be there. I believed in 12-step groups as much as I believed in feng shui, but I figured if I just sat and listened it wouldn't be so bad.

The meeting's topic was bottoming out—that moment when a person loses it so entirely that they finally acknowledge, "I need help." I wished I could go next door to the crack addicts' meeting. Surely their stories were more interesting than these endless tales of scarfing down batches of brownies and entire extra-large double-dough pizzas. Even the alcoholics in the rec room across the hall seemed to be laughing, but I was stuck with the fatties.

Finally, Tim was up. I looked at the floor as he catalogued a week of never stepping foot outside of his apartment and ordering a nonstop parade of pizzas, dim sum, pastas, and cheesecakes. He talked about the shame—not just of eating four extra-cheese, extra-pepperoni pizzas in the span of three hours—but of what he'd do to himself afterward. He'd go into the bathroom, and instead of, say, throwing up, he'd start hitting himself. Hard. Literally beating himself up. His wife had just announced that she was leaving him for another man.

As everyone clapped for Tim, I remembered the time as a preteen anorexic that I tried to cut the fat off my stomach with a pair of scissors. I thought about the shame and self-loathing and how similar Tim and I were on the inside, if not on the outside.

"Lori, would you like to share?" I heard the group leader ask.

I squirmed in my seat. "What?"

"You were nodding when Tim talked about hitting himself. Do you have anything to add?" Tim shot me a look that said, "You don't have to do this." But something about the strangeness of the setting—a David Lynch-esque freak show where suddenly I'd become the freak—made me want to tell the scissors story.

When I finished, nobody clapped but Tim. The rest of the room narrowed their eyes and stared at me, as if to say, "You, cutting the fat off your scrawny little stomach? Give me a break!" Even the leader, a 350-pound "bulimic, obsessive-compulsive binger," let out a sort of snicker before breaking the silence with, "Um, okay then. Thanks for sharing."

After the meeting, a woman with swollen cheeks approached me. "Excuse me," she said, resting her heavy hand on my shoulder. "I just want to warn you. Your neck may look healthy now, but if you keep throwing up, you'll ruin your glands."

"I don't throw up," I said.

"It's okay, honey," she said gently. "I didn't share for a long time either."

"No, really," I began, but the woman just shook her head and walked away.

I'd never before visited such an alternate universe, galaxies away from the land outside the rec room windows. It was a world in reverse, where the skinny girl was the odd girl out.

"It's too soon," I told Tim when he invited me to be his guest at his office retreat in the desert. I wasn't ready to hold hands in public, and I didn't think I could wear pockets all the time in ninety-degree weather.

"Why?" he asked, caressing my thighs as we lay on the floor by his fireplace. It was the first time we'd been back to his apartment since the refrigerator incident, and I noticed he'd taken the Julia Roberts photo down.

"It's just weird," I said. "I don't feel comfortable mixing my romantic life in a professional context like that."

"So let's go as friends. We'll get separate rooms and if I'm feeling 'friendly,' I'll even let you sleep in mine." I hesitated.

"Ah, c'mon," he smiled, hypnotizing me with his teeth. "You'll miss me if I'm away for four days."

He was right, but I couldn't imagine lying by the pool in a bikini next to Tim. Would he wear a bathing suit, or one of those awful terry-cloth getups? Would he be as shameless about his body with his colleagues as he was with me? Oddly, I was more self-conscious about his body than he was.

"Here, let's practice," he said, laughing. "Pretend we're at the retreat, and I'm introducing you around. I'll say, 'Melanie, this is my *friend* Lori.'"

"Who's Melanie?" I asked quickly.

"Oooh, my *friend* Lori seems jealous," Tim said.

"I am!" I remembered Tim's comment at the Italian restaurant, when he told me not to be embarrassed by the penis conversation: *Everyone wonders. At least the women who're interested.* Was it possible that other women saw in him what I did?

"Melanie's my boss, and a friend. But not a *friend* friend, like you." Tim started taking off my clothes. "See, I only make love with my *friend* friends. But I'll call you just plain 'friend' for short."

"Okay, I'll go as your 'friend,'" I said, kissing his cock.

"Tim never told me he had such a beautiful friend," a slick TV lawyer named Mike said at the office retreat's first dinner. For the rest of the weekend, Tim's single colleagues openly hit on me while the married ones—male and female—asked to set me up on dates back in L.A. Tim never had to say we were friends; people just assumed it. A 260-pound man and a 100-pound woman? It must have seemed so unlikely. I wondered if his colleagues could hear me scream through the walls when we fucked.

Part of me wanted to tell them, "Hey, your assumptions about this guy are insulting! Why can't an overweight guy get the girl? I'm standing by my men..." The slip made me giggle. *Stand by your men.* I couldn't stop laughing. What an asshole I was.

Or a coward.

"I just got out of a relationship," I'd tell people who

tried to set me up, and they'd hand me numbers for when I was "ready." Then, the last night, one of the firm's senior partners took me aside.

"Tim's our brightest young attorney," he said, sidling up to me by the dessert buffet. "And he's looking just great, getting in shape, don't you think?"

"Yeah," I agreed. "He's very disciplined."

He raised his right eyebrow. "You two are dating, aren't you?"

"Oh, no, see…" I looked around to make sure Tim was back at the table, drinking his decaf coffee, black. "We're just friends."

The partner shook his head. "Well, whatever you are, people don't drop a good fifty pounds so quickly out of nowhere. He's losing the weight for you, you know."

"Nah," I said. "He's losing it for him."

"You, him, doesn't matter. Fact is, he's losing it for love."

"Nah," I repeated lamely. But I worried he might be right.

In bed that night, I asked Tim why he started his diet. When I'd brought it up early on, he told me he'd begun dieting after his postdivorce depression lifted, which was before we met.

I never thought he was losing weight for me. Women routinely lose weight to please men, to ensure their love, but a man losing weight to please a woman? Who'd heard of such a thing?

Sweetie, are you still going to that aerobics class? Honey, you sure you want to eat that? No, you don't look fat, but maybe you'd feel better if you lost a little weight. All things women have heard, but men?

"I told you why," Tim said.

"Because you got over the breakup, right? Because you stopped feeling depressed?"

"Yeah," he said, tracing my spine with his tongue. I breathed a sigh of relief.

"I mean, let's face it," Tim continued between licks. "Who could be depressed knowing you?"

"Do you realize I've been in and out of a relationship since we last spoke?" Stella said indignantly when I called her back after two weeks of messages.

"I'm sorry, I've been busy," I said. "What happened?"

"Oh, he went back to his girlfriend. But it wouldn't have worked out anyway. I mean, he could fit into my jeans."

"So?"

"So?" she said, as if I had a brain injury. "So I'd always feel fat around him. Remember your fat guy? I'd like to date a fat guy, because I'd always be thinner than him. Women should date either fat guys or blind guys, then we wouldn't have to diet all the time."

"Or a fat blind guy—you could go nuts! Chocolate sundaes for breakfast, lunch and dinner!"

"I think I read that on a fortune cookie," Stella laughed. " 'For happy love life, date blind fat guy.' "

"Shoot, I gotta go," I said when I noticed Tim parking his car out front.

"Wait, how's the mystery guy?"

"Still mysterious," I said, watching Tim jog up the walk. He was starting to look almost normal, more like a bulky football player than a sumo wrestler. "But not for long."

Two weeks later, I got out of the shower and found Tim standing in my bedroom, staring at his hard-on.

"Happy to see me?" I asked.

"Look," he said, barely containing his excitement. "I *can* see my penis!" Tim examined it with the fascination of a twelve-year-old boy. "Hey, does it look...did I have a 300-pound dick and now it's just a 260-pound one?" he asked. "You know, the way breasts shrink when you lose weight?"

"Looks the same to me." I smiled. "I think all your carbs are being funneled to your groin."

At the eight-week mark, Tim weighed in at 255. By week twelve, he was down to 250. He was still at 250 four weeks later. His trainer thought he was starving so much that his body wouldn't lose any more fat, and suggested he be less rigid with his diet. So Tim agreed to get takeout again. We began a new routine after work—recapping our days, reading in bed, having sex, and ordering dinner. Then we'd spoon until it arrived. Cuddling with Tim was like being wrapped in a sheepskin comforter, all warm and soft and hairy. Gradually, I began to feel his muscles against my back.

We'd just finished making love when the doorbell rang. Tim threw on his sweats to pay for the food, but when he opened the door, it was Stella. And Amy and Kevin and Erica. Stella was holding a plate of cookies.

Everyone looked stunned. Tim stood there, shirtless, his huge gut naked.

"What are you doing here?" I asked from the hallway doorframe. The room smelled of candles and sex.

"We're doing an intervention," Stella said, unable to take her eyes off Tim. "We thought you were making up this whole guy thing to get us off your back."

"I'm Stella, by the way," she said to Tim. "Cookie?"

"No thanks, I'm on a..."

"*Stella*," I interrupted. "It's not a good time. Can I call you later?"

"Aren't you going to introduce us?" Stella asked. Amy and Erica waited expectantly while Kevin tried not to smirk. He was friends with my ex-boyfriend, and I knew he'd report back immediately: Lori's dating a fatty! She dumped you for *that*!

"This is Tim," I said quickly. "He's a friend and he's helping me with an article right now. I'll call you when we're done."

On the way out, they couldn't stop staring at Tim.

"Helping you with an article?" Tim said after they'd left. Small drops of moisture gathered in the corners of his eyes and suddenly he looked not fat but tiny, like a small wounded child.

I went over to hug him but the doorbell rang again: the delivery boy. A mushroom pizza for me, a dry salad for Tim.

"I'll take those," Tim said, walking with both packages past the delivery boy and out toward the sidewalk. "My *friend* back there—the half-naked one—she'll pay."

Tim didn't answer his phone that night. He later confessed that he'd been bingeing: my mushroom pizza, his green salad, a box of Oreos, a pound of See's candy, a package of bagels with cream cheese, and an artichoke. The artichoke only because it was the last food item left in his apartment. Now I knew what they meant in the OA meeting when they talked about "stuffing your anger by stuffing your face." By the time we spoke the next day, he said, his weight had shot up five pounds.

"Are we dating?" he asked. "Or are we friends?"

"I don't know," I mumbled.

"Well, by definition," he said, launching into lawyer mode, "we're more than friends. And if we're not, then we should stop doing things that friends don't do."

I thought about Stella's advice, the day after I met Tim: *for his sake, don't call.*

"I'd like to date," I said. "But I have to take things slowly. I'm still getting over my last relationship." We both knew this wasn't true. I hated myself. After all, I was the girl who wore no makeup, rarely bought clothes, and paid little attention to appearance. Or so I thought. When had I become so shallow?

"I think I can handle that...for now," Tim said. "But under one condition."

"What?

"Tell your friends that we're dating."

My friends were fascinated by the news. Some called me "brave" for seeing beyond the blubber and into Tim's soul. Others treated Tim like an alien creature, or a circus act. They all had questions: *Does he pig out at meals? Does he have a metabolism problem? A hormonal problem? How'd he marry someone who looks like Julia Roberts? Did she leave him because of the weight? Do you close your eyes when you have sex? Does he crush you? What positions are you in? How does it, y'know, work? Is he sweaty? Is he smelly? Does he fart a lot? Does he clog up your toilet? Can you get your arms around him?*

They didn't call Tim, Tim. Whenever they'd phone to see how we were doing, they'd ask, "How's the Fat Guy?" Or "Are you still getting lovin' from the Big Tub O' Goo?" These are the friends who say "mentally challenged" instead of "retarded" and get incensed if I use the term "Asian" instead of specifying that somebody is "Japanese" or "Korean." Fat, though, that's the last socially acceptable form of bigotry. Fat jokes are funny, even to my liberal politically correct friends.

"His name's Tim," I'd correct them.

"Oh, right. How's Tom?" they'd reply, not even realizing the slip.

I told them that Tim was losing weight, and that he had incredible willpower. Actually, though, his diet didn't seem to be going so well. Suddenly Tim began putting dressing on salads and eating bread at restaurants. He even dipped it in olive oil or added a pat of butter or two.

"Are you sure you want that butter?" I'd hear myself say. The more Tim went off his diet, the more I became the Food Nazi. It was like anorexia by proxy: *You're using mayonnaise? I thought you only used mustard. Two packets of sweetener? Aren't you only supposed to have one? Orange juice is fattening... it's all fructose.*

Tim also fired his trainer ("too expensive") and stopped working out each day. "I had a lot of work to do," he'd say. Or, "I only have time either to see you or to work out—you'd rather see me, right?"

"I'd rather that you work out, and get healthy again,"

I'd say. But we both knew what he was asking: would I love Tim if he stayed fat? And we both knew the answer.

Out in the world, I looked for couples like us. Somehow I thought I'd feel better if we weren't so unusual, if people didn't do double takes of us on the street. But not once did I see a lanky man walking arm in arm with an obese woman. Occasionally I'd see an overweight man with a thin, fit woman, but he'd always be much older and the woman assumed to be a wannabe starlet in it for the wealth or connections. The only other time I saw thin women with fat men was on family sitcoms, where the fat guy plays the affable, dopey husband and the wife the smart, sensible one who wears the pants. That wasn't Tim and me either.

Walking with Tim on a Sunday afternoon, though, I saw two figures up ahead—one wide and tubby, the other bony and small. They looked almost freakish, like a parody sketch from *Saturday Night Live*: the woman's thin arms hung from her sleeveless sundress, while the man's gleaming metal belt buckle accentuated his belly. It was a bright day, with sunlight reflecting off the glass buildings, and I couldn't see the couple clearly.

"Look," I said to Tim, pointing at the figures up ahead. "They're like us!"

Tim squinted at where I was pointing. "They *are* us," he said, shaking his head. As the fat man and skinny woman got closer, I realized he was right. I'd been watching our

reflections in the mirrored building ahead: MAN IN MIRROR
IS LARGER THAN HE APPEARS.

It was official: We didn't exist in nature.

"I love you," Tim whispered for the first time, a few
weeks later, after we'd had sex on my bedroom floor. Tim
had gained a good fifteen pounds so we'd gone back to the
floor for safety. His body was drenched in sweat, and his
breath smelled of bile. Billie Holiday's "What Is This
Thing Called Love" was on the CD player. *You took my love
and threw it away.*... I closed my eyes, pretending not to have
heard.

I remembered Holly Hunter's face in *Broadcast News,*
when Albert Brooks's character announces that he loves
her. "I love you," he tells her. "How about that—I buried
the lead?" and Holly Hunter's character actually cringes.
She doesn't love poor Albert. And I didn't love Tim. I
loved who he might have become.

"Did you hear what I said?" Tim asked, turning my
face toward his. His pores had gotten larger, probably from
the greasy junk food he'd been eating. His toned muscles
had returned to their dimpled fleshy state, which didn't so
much turn me off me as make me lose respect for him. It
was one thing when he was on a diet, when he mattered to
himself. It was another when he stopped caring.

"What?" I said, buying time. "I think I dozed off."

"Nothing," Tim said. "It's not important."

For the next several weeks, I tried to initiate Project Tim. I offered to work out with him, to take hikes, to help him plan his meals. He'd do okay for a few days, then go wild with Snickers or bags of barbecued potato chips.

"I'm getting back on track," he'd say sheepishly as I watched him wolf down a plate of fried calamari.

"Great, when?" I'd ask.

"Starting tomorrow. Remember what they tell us in OA—'take it one day at a time.'"

"That makes sense," I'd reply, shooting him a skeptical look. "But you haven't been to a meeting in a month."

I remembered seeing the thin picture of Tim on his refrigerator. Now I knew what he meant by the "cautionary tale" comment. What if, like his ex-wife, I didn't love him when he lost the weight? What if we just weren't right, and it had nothing to do with his size after all? If Tim stayed fat, he could say it was the weight—and he'd be right. He could say I had an irrational fear of fat and that I'd been the problem, not him. But if he got thin, and it didn't work out, he'd have to admit it was about something else. Something *in* him, something you can't just toss away, like the cocoon surrounding the butterfly.

"We have to talk," I said when Tim's weight shot back up to 280. It was like *Flowers for Algernon,* the famous story about a mentally retarded man made a genius by a brain operation, only to watch his intellectual capacity diminish to retardation again. Tim had miraculously lost 50 pounds, and now I watched in horror as he began to gain them all back. I felt responsible for his relapse.

"Why are you doing this?" I asked. "Is it because of me?"

"No," he said. "It's because of me. I realized you'd only love the thin me, and I don't want that."

Tim used food the way I had as an anorexic. Except that when I was feeling unloved and empty, I made myself feel emptier. It was masochistic, really. Tim, on the other hand, did the more logical thing. When he felt empty, he tried to fill himself up. To the tune of an extra 150 pounds. *Love all of me, or don't love me at all,* he seemed to be saying. And no matter how much I wanted to, I couldn't fall in love with his fleshy jowls and his 42-inch waist and his jiggling ass.

We never broke up officially. Five months after our first e-mails, we simply stopped sleeping together and at Tim's 300-pound mark, I began dating other men. They, too, had imperfections—some far worse than Tim's—but these flaws weren't visible to the naked eye. You can't see commitment-phobia, dumbness, narcissism, immaturity, or lack of humor the way you can see fat.

Those who heard about my experience told me it

shouldn't matter. If you really connect with him, they said, so what if the guy's fat—it's his heart that counts. Did they say this because the fat person in question happened to be a man? Would a man, for instance, ever be looked down on for balking at dating a "fat chick"? Would his friends say it's her heart that counts, and encourage him to be less shallow?

Recently, a friend told me about his colleague who was set up with a woman by mutual friends. They spoke on the phone, hit it off, and because they lived in different cities, decided to meet at a hotel in between. But when he got there, he saw that she was fat. Despite the weeks of daily three-hour phone calls, he couldn't get past her weight. He unceremoniously left the hotel that evening. In this same conversation, I heard about a woman who corresponded with a guy on an Internet dating service, and agreed to meet him in front of a restaurant. She waited for half an hour, saw the type of car he said he owned circle twice around the block, and then leave. She's sure it was because her online picture had been taken before she gained thirty pounds. She never heard from him again.

Was I so terrible for not wanting to date a fatty either?

"But he can lose the weight," Stella said one night, when I talked about how much I missed Tim's company.

He can, but he wants me to love him at any size. He doesn't think I should feel differently about him at 310 pounds or 280 or 160. I shouldn't, but I do. Bald, I can deal with. Short, I can deal with. A humongous nose, I can deal with. Missing a finger, fine. Facial scarring, okay. A few extra pounds, sure. But not an extra 150.

And it's not just because I was a teenage anorexic.

It makes me laugh when some of my friends say they'd date a fat guy. They insist that if they met an amazing man and he couldn't fit through a doorframe, it wouldn't be ideal, but it would be okay. They say I'm being closed-minded.

I think they're full of shit.

"Well, Tim's available," I've said to those friends who are single and constantly complaining that they can't find a good man.

Not one has asked for Tim's number.

IRVIN YALOM

Fat Lady

The world's finest tennis players train five hours a day to eliminate weaknesses in their game. Zen masters endlessly aspire to quiescence of the mind, the ballerina to consummate balance; and the priest forever examines his conscience. Every profession has within it a realm of possibility wherein the practitioner may seek perfection. For the psychotherapist that realm, that inexhaustible curriculum of self-improvement from which one never graduates, is referred to in the trade as countertransference. Where *transference* refers to feelings that the patient erroneously attaches ("transfers") to the therapist but that in fact originated out of earlier relationships, *countertransference* is the reverse—similar irrational feelings the therapist has toward the patient. Sometimes countertransference is dramatic and makes deep therapy impossible: imagine a Jew treating a Nazi, or a woman who has once been sexually assaulted treating a rapist. But, in milder form, countertransference insinuates itself into every course of psychotherapy.

The day Betty entered my office, the instant I saw her steering her ponderous two-hundred-fifty-pound, five-foot-two-inch frame toward my trim, high-tech office chair, I knew that a great trial of countertransference was in store for me.

I have always been repelled by fat women. I find them disgusting: their absurd sidewise waddle, their absence of body contour—breasts, laps, buttocks, shoulders, jawlines, cheekbones, *everything*, everything I like to see in a woman, obscured in an avalanche of flesh. And I hate their clothes—the shapeless, baggy dresses or, worse, the stiff elephantine blue jeans with the barrel thighs. How dare they impose that body on the rest of us?

The origins of these sorry feelings? I had never thought to inquire. So deep do they run that I never considered them prejudice. But were an explanation demanded of me, I suppose I could point to the family of fat, controlling women, including—featuring—my mother, who peopled my early life. Obesity, endemic in my family, was a part of what I had to leave behind when I, a driven, ambitious, first-generation American-born, decided to shake forever from my feet the dust of the Russian shtetl.

I can take other guesses. I have always admired, perhaps more than many men, the woman's body. No, not just admired: I have elevated, idealized, ecstacized it to a level and a goal that exceeds all reason. Do I resent the fat woman for her desecration of my desire, for bloating and profaning each lovely feature that I cherish? For stripping away my sweet illusion and revealing its base of flesh— flesh on the rampage?

I grew up in racially segregated Washington, D.C., the only son of the only white family in the midst of a black neighborhood. In the streets, the black attacked me for my whiteness, and in school, the white attacked me for my Jewishness. But there was always fatness, the fat kids, the big asses, the butts of jokes, those last chosen for athletic teams, those unable to run the circle of the athletic track. I needed someone to hate, too. Maybe that was where I learned it.

Of course, I am not alone in my bias. Cultural reinforcement is everywhere. Who ever has a kind word for the fat lady? But my contempt surpasses all cultural norms. Early in my career, I worked in a maximum security prison where the *least* heinous offense committed by any of my patients was a simple, single murder. Yet I had little difficulty accepting those patients, attempting to understand them, and finding ways to be supportive.

But when I see a fat lady eat, I move down a couple of rungs on the ladder of human understanding. I want to tear the food away. To push her face into the ice cream. "Stop stuffing yourself! Haven't you had enough, for Chrissakes?" I'd like to wire her jaws shut!

Poor Betty—thank God, thank God—knew none of

this as she innocently continued her course toward my chair, slowly lowered her body, arranged her folds and, with her feet not quite reaching the floor, looked up at me expectantly.

Now why, thought I, do her feet not reach the ground? She's not that short. She sat high in the chair, as though she were sitting in her own lap. Could it be that her thighs and buttocks are so inflated that her feet have to go farther to reach the floor? I quickly swept this conundrum from my mind—after all, this person had come to seek help from me. A moment later, I found myself thinking of the little fat woman cartoon figure in the movie *Mary Poppins*— the one who sings "Supercalifragilisticexpialidocious"—for that was who Betty reminded me of. With an effort I swept that away as well. And so it went: the entire hour with her was an exercise of my sweeping from my mind one derogatory thought after another in order to offer her my full attention. I fantasized Mickey Mouse, the sorcerer's apprentice in *Fantasia,* sweeping away my distracting thoughts until I had to sweep away that image, too, in order to attend to Betty.

As usual, I began to orient myself with demographic questions. Betty informed me that she was twenty-seven and single, that she worked in public relations for a large New York–based retail chain which, three months ago, had transferred her to California for eighteen months to assist in the opening of a new franchise.

She had grown up, an only child, on a small, poor

ranch in Texas where her mother has lived alone since her father's death fifteen years ago. Betty was a good student, attended the state university, went to work for a department store in Texas, and after two years was transferred to the central office in New York. Always overweight, she became markedly obese in late adolescence. Aside from two or three brief periods when she lost forty to fifty pounds on crash diets, she had hovered between two hundred and two hundred fifty since she was twenty-one.

I got down to business and asked my standard opening question: "What ails?"

"Everything," Betty replied. Nothing was going right in her life. In fact, she said, she had no life. She worked sixty hours a week, had no friends, no social life, no activities in California. Her life, such as it was, she said, was in New York, but to request a transfer now would doom her career, which was already in jeopardy because of her unpopularity with co-workers. Her company had originally trained her, along with eight other novices, in a three-month intensive course. Betty was preoccupied that she was neither performing nor progressing through promotions as well as her eight classmates. She lived in a furnished suburban apartment doing nothing, she said, but working and eating and chalking off the days till her eighteen months were up.

A psychiatrist in New York, Dr. Farber, whom she saw for approximately four months, had treated her with antidepressant medication. Though she continued to take it, it had not helped her: she was deeply depressed, cried every evening, wished she were dead, slept fitfully, and always awoke by four or five A.M. She moped around the house and on Sundays, her day off, never dressed and spent the day eating sweets in front of the television set. The week before, she had phoned Dr. Farber, who gave her my name and suggested she call for a consultation.

"Tell me more about what you're struggling with in your life," I asked.

"My eating is out of control," Betty said, chuckling, and added, "You could say my eating is always out of control, but now it is *really* out of control. I've gained around twenty pounds in the past three months, and I can't get into most of my clothes."

That surprised me, her clothes seeming so formless, so infinitely expandable, that I couldn't imagine them being outdistanced.

"Other reasons why you decided to come in just now?"

"I saw a medical doctor last week for headaches, and he told me that my blood pressure is dangerously high, around 220 over 110, and that I've got to begin to lose weight. He seemed upset. I don't know how seriously to take him—everyone in California is such a health nut. He wears jeans and running shoes in his office."

She uttered all these things in a gay chatty tone, as though she were talking about someone else, or as though she and I were college sophomores swapping stories in a dorm some rainy Sunday afternoon. She tried to poke me into joining the fun. She told jokes. She had a gift for imitating accents and mimicked her laid-back Marin County physician, her Chinese customers, and her Midwestern boss. She must have laughed twenty times during the session, her high spirits apparently in no way dampened by my stern refusal to be coerced into laughing with her.

I always take very seriously the business of entering into a treatment contract with a patient. Once I accept someone for treatment, I commit myself to stand by that person: to spend all the time and all the energy that proves necessary for the patient's improvement; and most of all, to relate to the patient in an intimate, authentic manner.

But could I relate to Betty? To be frank, she revolted me. It was an effort for me to locate her face, so layered and swathed in flesh as it was. Her silly commentary was equally offputting. By the end of our first hour, I felt irritated and bored. Could I be intimate with her? I could scarcely think of a single person with whom I *less* wished to be intimate. But this was *my* problem, not Betty's. It was time, after twenty-five years of practice, for me to change. Betty represented the ultimate countertransference challenge—and, for that very reason, I offered then and there to be her therapist.

Surely no one can be critical of a therapist striving to improve his technique. But what, I wondered uneasily, about the rights of the patient? Is there not a difference between a therapist scrubbing away unseemly countertransference stains and a dancer or a Zen master striving for perfection in each of those disciplines? It is one thing to improve one's backhand service return but quite another to sharpen one's skills at the expense of some fragile, troubled person.

These thoughts all occurred to me but I found them dismissible. It was true that Betty offered an opportunity to improve my personal skills as a therapist. It was, however, also true that my future patients would benefit from whatever growth I would attain. Besides, human service professionals have always practiced on the living patient. There is no alternative. How could medical education, to take one example, survive without student clinical clerkships? Furthermore, I have always found that responsible neophyte therapists who convey their sense of curiosity and enthusiasm often form excellent therapeutic relationships and can be as effective as a seasoned professional.

It's the relationship that heals, the relationship that heals, the relationship that heals—my professional rosary. I say that often to students. And say other things as well, about the way to relate to a patient—positive unconditional regard, nonjudgmental acceptance, authentic engagement, empathic understanding. How was I going to be able to heal Betty through our relationship? How authentic, empathic, or accepting could I be? How honest? How would I respond when she asked about my feelings toward her? It was my hope that I would change as Betty and I progressed in her (our) therapy. For the time being, it seemed to me that Betty's social interactions were so primitive and superficial that no penetrating therapist-patient relationship analysis would be necessary.

I had secretly hoped that her appearance would be off-set in some way by her interpersonal characteristics—that is, by the sheer vivacity or mental agility I have found in a few fat women—but that, alas, was not to be. The better I knew her, the more boring and superficial she seemed.

During the first few sessions, Betty described, in endless detail, problems she encountered at work with customers, co-workers, and bosses. She often, despite my inner groans, described some particularly banal conversation by playing several of the roles—I've always hated that. She described, again in tedious detail, all the attractive men at work and the minute, pathetic machinations she'd go through to exchange a few sentences with them. She resisted every effort on my part to dip beneath the surface.

Not only was our initial, tentative "cocktail chatter" indefinitely prolonged, but I had a strong sense that, even when we got past this stage, we would remain fused to the surface of things—that as long as Betty and I met, we were doomed to talk about pounds, diets, petty work grievances, and the reasons she did not join an aerobics class. Good Lord, what had I gotten myself into?

Every one of my notes of these early sessions contains phrases such as: "Another boring session"; "Looked at the clock about every three minutes today"; "The most boring patient I have ever seen"; "Almost fell asleep today—had to sit up in my chair to stay awake"; "Almost fell off my chair today."

While I was considering shifting to a hard, uncomfortable chair, it suddenly occurred to me that when I was in therapy with Rollo May, he used to sit in a straight-backed wooden chair. He said he had a bad back, but I knew him well for many years afterward and never heard him mention back trouble. Could it be that he found *me*—?

Betty mentioned that she hadn't liked Dr. Farber because he often fell asleep during their hour. Now I knew why! When I spoke to Dr. Farber on the phone, he did not mention his naps, of course, but he did volunteer that Betty had not been able to learn how to use therapy. It was not hard to understand why he had started her on medication; we psychiatrists so often resort to that when we cannot get anything going in therapy.

Where to start? How to start? I struggled to find some handhold. It was pointless to begin by addressing her weight. Betty made it clear immediately that she hoped therapy would help her get to the point where she could seriously consider weight reduction, but she was a long way from that at this time. "When I'm this depressed, eating is the only thing that keeps me going."

But when I focused on her depression, she presented a persuasive case that depression was an appropriate response to her life situation. Who wouldn't feel depressed holed up in a small furnished apartment in an impersonal

California suburb for eighteen months, torn away from one's real life—one's home, social activities, friends?

So I then attempted to help her work on her life situation, but I could make little headway. She had plenty of daunting explanations. She didn't make friends easily, she pointed out: no obese woman does. (On that point I needed no persuasion.) People in California had their own tight cliques and did not welcome strangers. Her only social contacts were at work, where most of her co-workers resented her supervisory role. Besides, like all Californians, they were jocks—into surfing and skydiving. Could I see her doing that? I swept away a fantasy of her slowly sinking on a surfboard and acknowledged she had a point—those did not seem to be her sports.

What other options were there? she asked. The singles world is impossible for obese people. To prove that point, she described a desperation date she had had the month before—her only date in years. She answered an ad in the personal section of *The Bay Guardian*, a local newspaper. Although most of the ads placed by men explicitly specified a "slim" woman, one did not. She called and arranged to go out to dinner with a man named George, who asked her to wear a rose in her hair and to meet him in the bar of a local restaurant.

His face fell, she reported, when he first caught sight of her, but, to his everlasting credit, he acknowledged that he was indeed George and then behaved like a gentleman throughout dinner. Though Betty never again heard from George, she often thought about him. On several other such attempts in the past, she had been stood up by men who probably spotted her from afar and left without speaking to her.

In some desperation, I stretched for ways to be helpful to Betty. Perhaps (in an effort to conceal my negative feelings) I tried too hard, and I made the beginner's mistake of suggesting other options. Had she considered the Sierra Club? No, she lacked the stamina for hiking. Or Overeaters Anonymous, which might provide some social network. No, she hated groups. Other suggestions met a similar fate. There had to be some other way.

The first step in all therapeutic change is responsibility assumption. If one feels in no way responsible for one's predicament, then how can one change it? That was precisely the situation with Betty: she completely externalized the problem. It was not *her* doing: it was the work transfer, or the sterile California culture, or the absence of cultural events, or the jock social scene, or society's miserable attitude toward obese people. Despite my best efforts, Betty denied any personal contribution to her unhappy life situation.

Oh yes, she could, on an intellectual level, agree that, if she stopped eating and lost weight, the world might treat her differently. But that was too far removed from her, too long term, and her eating seemed too much out of her control. Besides she marshaled other responsibility-absolving arguments: the genetic component (there was considerable obesity on both sides of her family); and the new research demonstrating physiological abnormalities in the obese, ranging from lower basal metabolic rates to a preset, programmed, relatively uninfluenceable body weight. No, that would not work. Ultimately I would have to help her assume responsibility for her appearance—but saw no leverage for achieving that at this time. I had to start with something more immediate. I knew a way.

The psychotherapist's single most valuable practical tool is the "process" focus. Think of *process* as opposed to *content*. In a conversation, the content consists of the actual words uttered, the substantive issues discussed; the process, however, is *how* the content is expressed and especially what this mode of expression reveals about the relationship between the participating individuals.

What I had to do was to get away from the content—to stop, for example, attempting to provide simplistic solutions to Betty—and to focus on process—on how we were relating to each other. And there was one outstanding characteristic of our relationship—*boredom*. And that is precisely where countertransference complicates things: I had to be clear about how much of the boredom was *my* problem, about how bored I would be with *any* fat woman.

So I proceeded cautiously—too cautiously. My negative feelings slowed me down. I was too afraid of making my aversion visible. I would never have waited so long with a patient I liked more. I spurred myself to get moving. If I were going to be helpful to Betty, I had to sort out, to trust, and to act upon my feelings.

The truth was that this was a very boring lady, and I needed to confront her with that in some acceptable way. She could deny responsibility for anything else—the absence of friends in her current life, the tough singles scene, the horrors of suburbia—but I was *not* going to let her deny responsibility for boring me.

I dared not utter the word *boring*—far too vague and too pejorative. I needed to be precise and constructive. I asked myself what, exactly, was boring about Betty, and identified two obvious characteristics. First of all, she never revealed anything intimate about herself. Second, there was her damned giggling, her forced gaiety, her reluctance to be appropriately serious.

It would be difficult to make her aware of these characteristics without hurting her. I decided upon a general strategy: my basic position would be that I wanted to get closer to her but that her behavioral traits got in the way. I thought it would be difficult for her to take offense with any criticism of her behavior when framed in that context. She could only be pleased at my wanting to know her better. I decided to start with her lack of self-revelation and, toward the end of a particularly soporific session, took the plunge.

"Betty, I'll explain later why I'm asking you this, but I'd like you to try something new today. Would you give yourself a score from one to ten on how much revealing about yourself you've done during our hour together today? Consider ten to be the most significant revealing you can imagine and one to be the type of revealing you might do, let's say, with strangers in a line at the movies."

A mistake. Betty spent several minutes explaining why she wouldn't go to the movies alone. She imagined people pitied her for having no friends. She sensed their dread that she might crowd them by sitting next to them. She saw the curiosity, the bemusement in their faces as they watched to see whether she could squeeze into a single narrow movie seat. When she began to digress further—extending the discussion to airline seats and how seated passengers' faces grew white with fear when she started down the aisle searching for her seat—I interrupted her, repeated my request, and defined "one" as "casual conversation at work."

Betty responded by giving herself a "ten." I was astonished (I had expected a "two" or "three") and told her so. She defended her rating on the basis that she had told me things she had never shared before: that, for example, she had once stolen a magazine from a drugstore and was fearful about going alone to a restaurant or to the movies.

We repeated that same scenario several times. Betty insisted she was taking huge risks, yet, as I said to her, "Betty, you rate yourself 'ten,' yet it didn't *feel* that way to me. It didn't feel that you were taking a real risk with me."

"I have never told anybody else these things. Not Dr. Farber, for example."

"How do you feel telling me these things?"

"I feel fine doing it."

"Can you use other words than *fine*? It must be scary or liberating to say these things for the first time!"

"I feel O.K. doing it. I know you're listening professionally. It's O.K. I feel O.K. I don't know what you want."

"How can you be so sure I'm listening professionally? You have no doubts?"

Careful, careful! I couldn't promise more honesty than I was willing to give. There was no way that she could deal with my revelation of negative feelings. Betty denied any doubts—and at this point told me about Dr. Farber's falling asleep on her and added that I seemed much more interested than he.

What *did* I want from her? From *her* standpoint she was revealing much. I had to be sure I really knew. What was there about her revealing that left me unmoved? It struck me that she was always revealing something that occurred elsewhere—another time, another place. She was incapable, or unwilling, to reveal herself in the immediate present that we two were sharing. Hence, her evasive response of "O.K." or "Fine" whenever I asked about her here-and-now feelings.

That was the first important discovery I made about Betty: she was desperately isolated, and she survived this isolation only by virtue of the sustaining myth that her intimate life was being lived elsewhere. Her friends, her circle of acquaintances, were not here, but elsewhere, in New York, in Texas, in the past. In fact, everything of importance was elsewhere. It was at this time that I first began to suspect that for Betty there was no "here" there.

Another thing: if she was revealing more of herself to me than to anyone before, then what was the nature of her close relationships? Betty responded that she had a reputation for being easy to talk to. She and I, she said, were in the same business: she was everyone's therapist. She added that she had a lot of friends, but no one knew *her*. Her trademark was that she listened well and was entertaining. She hated the thought, but the stereotype was true: she was the jolly fat woman.

This led naturally into the other primary reason I found Betty so boring: she was acting in bad faith with me—in our face-to-face talks she was never real, she was all pretense and false gaiety.

"I'm really interested in what you said about being, or rather pretending to be, jolly. I think you are determined, absolutely committed, to be jolly with me."

"Hmmm, interesting theory, Dr. Watson."

"You've done this since our first meeting. You tell me about a life that is full of despair, but you do it in a bouncy 'aren't-we-having-a-good-time?' way."

"That's the way I am."

"When you stay jolly like that, I lose sight of how much pain you're having."

"That's better than wallowing in it."

"But you come here for help. Why is it so necessary for you to entertain me?"

Betty flushed. She seemed staggered by my confrontation and retreated by sinking into her body. Wiping her brow with a tiny handkerchief, she stalled for time.

"Zee suspect takes zee fifth."

"Betty, I'm going to be persistent today. What would happen if you stopped trying to entertain me?"

"I don't see anything wrong with having some fun. Why take everything so...so...I don't know— You're always so serious. Besides, this is me, this is the way I am. I'm not sure I know what you're talking about. What do you mean by my entertaining you?"

"Betty, this is important, the most important stuff we've gotten into so far. But you're right. First, you've got to know exactly what I mean. Would it be O.K. with you if, from now on in our future sessions, I interrupt and point out when you're entertaining me—the moment it occurs?"

Betty agreed—she could hardly refuse me; and I now had at my disposal an enormously liberating device. I was now permitted to interrupt her instantaneously (reminding her, of course, of our new agreement) whenever she giggled, adopted a silly accent, or attempted to amuse me or to make light of things in any distracting way.

Within three or four sessions, her "entertaining" behavior disappeared as she, for the first time, began to speak of her life with the seriousness it deserved. She reflected that she had to be entertaining to keep others interested in her. I commented that, in this office, the opposite was true:

the more she tried to entertain me, the more distant and less interested I felt.

But Betty said she didn't know how else to be: I was asking her to dump her entire social repertoire. Reveal herself? If she were to reveal herself, what would she show? There was nothing there inside. She was empty. (The word *empty* was to arise more and more frequently as therapy proceeded. Psychological "emptiness" is a common concept in the treatment of those with eating disorders.)

I supported her as much as possible at this point. *Now*, I pointed out to Betty, she was taking risks. *Now* she was up to eight or nine on the revealing scale. Could she feel the difference? She got the point quickly. She said she felt frightened, like jumping out of a plane without a parachute.

I was less bored now. I looked at the clock less frequently and once in a while checked the time during Betty's hour not, as before, to count the number of minutes I had yet to endure, but to see whether sufficient time remained to open up a new issue.

Nor was it necessary to sweep from my mind derogatory thoughts about her appearance. I no longer noticed her body and, instead, looked into her eyes. In fact, I noted with surprise the first stirrings of empathy within me. When Betty told me about going to a western bar where two rednecks sidled up behind her and mocked her by mooing like a cow, I felt outraged for her and told her so.

My new feelings toward Betty caused me to recall, and to be ashamed of, my initial response to her. I cringed when I reflected on all the other obese women whom I had related to in an intolerant and dehumanized fashion.

These changes all signified that we were making progress: we were successfully addressing Betty's isolation and her hunger for closeness. I hoped to show her that another person could know her fully and still care for her.

Betty now felt definitely engaged in therapy. She thought about our discussions between sessions, had long imaginary conversations with me during the week, looked forward to our meetings, and felt angry and disappointed when business travel caused her to miss meetings.

But at the same time she became unaccountably more distressed and reported more sadness and more anxiety. I pounced at the opportunity to understand this development. Whenever the patient begins to develop symptoms in respect to the relationship with the therapist, therapy has really begun, and inquiry into these symptoms will open the path to the central issues.

Her anxiety had to do with her fear of getting too dependent or addicted to therapy. Our sessions had become the most important thing in her life. She didn't know what would happen to her if she didn't have her weekly "fix." It seemed to me she was still resisting closeness by referring to a "fix" rather than to me, and I gradually confronted her on that point.

"Betty, what's the danger in letting me matter to you?"

"I'm not sure. It feels scary, like I'll need you too much. I'm not sure you'll be there for me. I'm going to have to leave California in a year, remember."

"A year's a long time. So you avoid me now because you won't always have me?"

"I know it doesn't make sense. But I do the same thing with California. I like New York and I don't want to like California. I'm afraid that, if I form friends here and start to like it, I might not want to leave. The other thing is that I start to feel, 'Why bother?' I'm here for such a short time. Who wants temporary friendships?"

"The problem with that attitude is you end up with an unpeopled life. Maybe that's part of the reason you feel empty inside. One way or another, every relationship must end. There's no such thing as a lifetime guarantee. It's like refusing to enjoy watching the sun rise because you hate to see it set."

"It sounds crazy when you put it like that, but that's what I do. When I meet a new person whom I like, I start right away to imagine what it will be like to say goodbye to them."

I knew this was an important issue, and that we would return to it. Otto Rank described this life stance with a wonderful phrase: "Refusing the loan of life in order to avoid the debt of death."

Betty now entered into a depression which was short-lived and had a curious, paradoxical twist. She was enlivened by the closeness and the openness of our interaction; but, rather than allow herself the enjoyment of that feeling, she was saddened by the realization that her life heretofore had been so devoid of intimacy.

I was reminded of another patient I had treated the year before, a forty-four-year-old excessively responsible, conscientious physician. One evening in the midst of a marital dispute, she uncharacteristically drank too much, went out of control, threw plates against the wall, and narrowly missed her husband with a lemon pie. When I saw her two days later, she seemed guilty and depressed. In an effort to console her, I tried to suggest that losing control is not always a catastrophe. But she interrupted and told me I had misunderstood: she felt no guilt but was instead overcome with regret that she had waited until she was forty-four to relinquish her controls and let some real feelings out.

Despite her two hundred and fifty pounds, Betty and I had rarely discussed her eating and her weight. She had often talked about epic (and invariably unproductive) struggles she had had with her mother and with other friends who tried to help her control her eating. I was determined to avoid that role; instead, I placed my faith in the assumption that, if I could help remove the obstacles that lay in her path, Betty would, on her own, take the initiative to care for her body.

So far, by addressing her isolation, I had already cleared away major obstacles: Betty's depression had lifted; and, having established a social life for herself, she no longer regarded food as her sole source of satisfaction. But it was not until she stumbled upon an extraordinary revelation about the dangers of losing weight that she could make the decision to begin her diet. It came about in this way.

When she had been in therapy for a few months, I decided that her progress would be accelerated if she worked in a therapy group as well as in individual therapy. For one thing, I was certain it would be wise to establish a supportive community to help sustain her in the difficult diet days yet to come. Furthermore, a therapy group would provide Betty an opportunity to explore the interpersonal issues we had opened up in our therapy—the concealment, the need to entertain, the feeling she had nothing to offer. Though Betty was very frightened and initially resisted my suggestion, she gamely agreed and entered a therapy group led by two psychiatric residents.

One of her first group meetings happened to be a highly unusual session in which Carlos, also in individual therapy with me, informed the group of his incurable cancer. Betty's father had died of cancer when she was twelve, and since then she had been terrified of the disease. In college she had initially elected a premedical curriculum but gave it up for fear of being in contact with cancer patients.

Over the next few weeks, the contact with Carlos generated so much anxiety in Betty that I had to see her in several emergency sessions and had difficulty persuading her to continue in the group. She developed distressing physical symptoms—including headaches (her father died of brain cancer), backaches, and shortness of breath—and was tormented with the obsessive thought that she, too, had cancer. Since she was phobic about seeing doctors (because of her shame about her body, she rarely permitted a physical exam and had never had a pelvic exam), it was hard to reassure her about her health.

Witnessing Carlos's alarming weight loss reminded Betty of how, over a twelve-month period, she had watched her father shrink from an obese man to a skeleton wrapped in great folds of spare skin. Though she acknowledged that it was an irrational thought, Betty realized that since her father's death she had believed that weight loss would make her susceptible to cancer.

She had strong feelings about hair loss as well. When she first joined the group, Carlos (who had lost his hair as a result of chemotherapy) was wearing a toupee, but the day he informed the group about his cancer, he came bald to the meeting. Betty was horrified, and visions of her father's baldness—he had been shaven for his brain surgery—returned to her. She remembered also how frightened she had been when, on previous strenuous diets, she herself had suffered considerable hair loss.

These disturbing feelings had vastly compounded Betty's weight problems. Not only did food represent her sole form of gratification, not only was it a method of assuaging her feeling of emptiness, not only did thinness evoke the pain of her father's death, but she felt, unconsciously, that losing weight would result in *her* death.

Gradually Betty's acute anxiety subsided. She had never before talked openly about these issues: perhaps the sheer catharsis helped; perhaps it was useful for her to recognize the magical nature of her thinking; perhaps some of her horrifying thoughts were simply desensitized by talking about them in the daylight in a calm, rational manner.

During this time, Carlos was particularly helpful. Betty's parents had, until the very end, denied the seriousness of her father's illness. Such massive denial always plays havoc with the survivors, and Betty had neither been prepared for his death nor had the opportunity to say goodbye. But Carlos modeled a very different approach to his fate: he was courageous, rational, and open with his feelings about his illness and his approaching death. Furthermore, he was especially kind to Betty—perhaps it was that he knew she was my patient, perhaps that she came along when he was in a generous ("everybody has got a heart") state of mind, perhaps simply that he always had a fondness for fat women (which, I regret to say, I had always considered further proof of his perversity).

Betty must have felt that the obstructions to losing weight had been sufficiently removed because she gave unmistakable evidence that a major campaign was about to be launched. I was astonished by the scope and complexity of the preparatory arrangements.

First, she enrolled in an eating-disorder program at the clinic where I worked and completed their demanding protocol, which included a complex physical workup (she still refused a pelvic exam) and a battery of psychological tests. She then cleared her apartment of food—every can, every package, every bottle. She made plans for alternative social activities: she pointed out to me that eliminating lunches and dinners puts a crimp into one's social calendar. To my surprise, she joined a square-dancing group (this lady's got guts, I thought) and a weekly bowling league—her father had often taken her bowling when she was a child, she explained. She bought a used stationary bicycle and set it up in front of her TV set. She then said her goodbyes to old friends—her last Granny Goose Hawaiian-style potato chip, her last Mrs. Fields chocolate chip cookie, and, toughest of all, her last honey-glazed doughnut.

There was considerable internal preparation as well, which Betty found difficult to describe other than to say she was "gathering inner resolve" and waiting for the right moment to commence the diet. I grew impatient and amused myself with a vision of an enormous Japanese sumo wrestler pacing, posturing, and grunting himself into readiness.

Suddenly she was off! She went on a liquid Optifast diet, ate no solid food, bicycled forty minutes every morning, walked three miles every afternoon, and bowled and square-danced once a week. Her fatty casing began to disintegrate. She began to shed bulk. Great chunks of overhanging flesh broke off and were washed away. Soon the pounds flowed off in rivulets—two, three, four, sometimes five pounds a week.

Betty started each hour with a progress report: ten pounds lost, then twenty, twenty-five, thirty. She was down to two hundred forty pounds, then two hundred thirty, and two hundred twenty. It seemed astonishingly fast and easy. I was delighted for her and commended her strongly each week on her efforts. But in those first weeks I was also aware of an uncharitable voice within me, a voice saying, "Good God, if she's losing it that fast, think of how much food she must have been putting away!"

The weeks passed, the campaign continued. After three months, she weighed in at two hundred ten. Then two hundred, a fifty-pound loss! Then one hundred ninety. The opposition stiffened. Sometimes she came into my office in tears after a week without food and no compensating weight loss. Every pound put up a fight, but Betty stayed on the diet.

Those were ghastly months. She hated everything. Her life was a torment—the disgusting liquid food, the stationary bicycle, the hunger pangs, the diabolic McDonald's hamburger ads on television, and the smells, the ubiquitous smells: popcorn in the movies, pizza in the bowling alley, croissants in the shopping center, crab at Fisherman's Wharf. Was there nowhere in the world an odor-free place?

Every day was a bad day. Nothing in her life gave her pleasure. Others in the eating-disorder clinic's weight-reduction group gave up—but Betty hung tough. My respect for her grew.

I like to eat, too. Often I look forward all day to a

special meal; and, when the craving strikes, no obstacle can block my way to the dim sum restaurant or the gelato stand. But as Betty's ordeal continued, I began to feel guilty eating—as though I were acting in bad faith toward her. Whenever I sat down to eat pizza or pasta al pesto or enchiladas con salsa verde or German-chocolate-cake ice cream, or any other special treat I knew Betty liked, I thought of her. I shuddered when I thought of her dining, can opener in hand, on Optifast liquid. Sometimes I passed up seconds in her honor.

It happened that, during this period, I passed the upper weight limit I allow myself, and went on a three-week diet. Since my diets consist primarily of eliminating ice cream and French fries, I could hardly say to Betty that I was joining hands with her in a sympathy fast. Nonetheless, during these three weeks I felt her deprivation more keenly. I was moved now when she told me how she cried herself to sleep. I ached for her when she described the starving child within her howling, "Feed me! Feed me!"

One hundred eighty. One hundred seventy. An eighty-pound weight loss! Betty's mood now fluctuated wildly, and I grew increasingly concerned for her. She had occasional brief periods of pride and exhilaration (especially when she went shopping for slimmer clothing), but mainly she experienced such deep despondency that it was all she could do to get herself to work each morning.

At times she grew irritable and raised several old grievances with me. Had I referred her to a therapy group as a way of dumping her or, at least, sharing the load and getting her partly off my hands? Why had I not asked her more about her eating habits? After all, eating was her life. Love her, love her eating. (Careful, careful, she's getting close.) Why had I agreed with her when she listed the reasons that medical school was not possible for her (her age, lack of stamina, laziness, having taken few of the prerequisite courses, and lack of funds)? She viewed, she told me now, my suggestion about a possible career in nursing as a putdown, and accused me of saying, "The girl's not smart enough for medical school—so let her be a nurse!"

At times, she was petulant and regressed. Once, for example, when I inquired about why she had become inactive in her therapy group, she simply glared and refused to answer. When I pressed her to say exactly what was on her mind, she said in a singsong child's voice, "If I can't have a cookie, I won't do anything for you."

During one of her depressed periods, she had a vivid dream.

I was in a place like Mecca where people go to commit suicide legally. I was with a close friend but I don't remember who. She was going to commit suicide by jumping down a deep tunnel. I promised her I'd retrieve her body but, later, I realized that to do this I'd have to crawl down this terrible tunnel with all sorts of dead and decaying bodies around and I didn't think I could do it.

In associating to this dream Betty said that, earlier the day of the dream, she had been thinking that she had shed a whole body: she had lost eighty pounds, and there was a woman in her office who weighed only eighty pounds. At the time she had imagined granting an autopsy and holding a funeral for the "body" she had shed. This macabre thought, Betty suspected, was echoed in the dream image of retrieving her friend's dead body from the tunnel.

The imagery and depth of the dream brought home to me how far she had come. It was hard to remember the giggling, superficial woman of a few months before. Betty had my full attention for every minute of every session now. Who could have imagined that, out of that woman whose vacuous chatter had so bored me and her previous psychiatrist, this thoughtful, spontaneous, and sensitive person could have emerged?

One hundred sixty-five. Another kind of emergence was taking place. One day in my office I looked over at Betty and noticed, for the first time, that she had a lap. I looked again. Had it always been there? Maybe I was paying more attention to her now. I didn't think so: her body contour, from chin to toes, had always been smoothly globular. A couple of weeks later, I saw definite signs of a breast, two breasts. A week later, a jawline, then a chin, an elbow. It was all there—there had been a person, a handsome woman, buried in there all the time.

Others, especially men, had noticed the change, and now touched and poked her during conversations. A man at the office walked her out to her car. Her hairdresser, gratuitously, gave her a scalp massage. She was certain her boss was eyeing her breasts.

One day Betty announced, "one hundred fifty-nine," and added that this was "virgin territory"—that is, she hadn't weighed in the one hundred fifties since high school. Though my response—asking whether she worried about entering "nonvirgin territory"—was a sorry joke, it nonetheless initiated an important discussion about sex.

Though she had an active sexual fantasy life, she had never had any physical contact with a man—not a hug, not a kiss, not even a lascivious grab. She had always craved sex and was angry that society's attitude toward the obese sentenced her to sexual frustration. Only now, when she was approaching a weight when sexual invitations might materialize, only now when her dreams teemed with menacing male figures (a masked doctor plunging a large hypodermic needle into her abdomen, a leering man peeling the scab off a large abdominal wound), did she recognize that she was very frightened of sex.

These discussions released a flood of painful memories about a lifetime of rejection by males. She had never been asked on a date and never attended a school dance or party. She played the confidante role very well and had helped many friends plan their weddings. They were just about all married off now, and she could no longer conceal from herself that she would forever play the role of the unchosen observer.

We soon moved from sex into the deeper waters of her basic sexual identity. Betty had heard that her father had really wanted a son and been silently disappointed when she was born. One night she had two dreams about a lost twin brother. In one dream she and he wore identification badges and kept switching them with each other. She finished him off in another dream: he squeezed into a crowded elevator into which she couldn't fit (because of her size). Then the elevator crashed, killing all the passengers, and she was left sifting through his remains.

In another dream, her father gave her a horse called "She's a Lady." She had always wanted a horse from him, and in the dream not only was that childhood wish fulfilled but her father officially christened her a lady.

Our discussions about sexual practice and her sexual identity generated so much anxiety and such an agonizing sense of emptiness that, on several occasions, she binged on cookies and doughnuts. By now Betty was permitted some solid food—one diet TV dinner a day—but found this more difficult to follow than the liquid-only diet.

Looming ahead was an important symbolic marker—the loss of the one-hundredth pound. This specific goal, never to be attained, had powerful sexual connotations. For one thing Carlos had, months before, only half jokingly told Betty he was going to take her to Hawaii for a weekend when she had lost a hundred pounds. Furthermore, as part of her pre-diet mental preparation, Betty had vowed herself that when she lost a hundred pounds she was going

to contact George, the man whose personal ad she had answered, to surprise him with her new body and reward his
gentlemanly behavior with her sexual favors.

In an effort to reduce her anxiety, I urged moderation
and suggested she approach sex with less drastic steps: for
example, by spending time talking to men; by educating herself about such topics as sexual anatomy, sexual mechanics,
and masturbation. I recommended reading material and
urged her to visit a female gynecologist and to explore these
issues with her girlfriends and her therapy group.

Throughout this period of rapid weight loss, another
extraordinary phenomenon was taking place. Betty experienced emotional flashbacks and would spend much of a
therapy hour tearfully discussing startlingly vivid memories,
such as the day she left Texas to move to New York, or her
college graduation, or her anger at her mother for being
too timid and fearful to attend her high school graduation.

At first it seemed that these flashbacks, as well as the
accompanying extreme mood swings, were chaotic, random occurrences; but after several weeks, Betty realized
that they were following a coherent pattern: as she lost
weight she *re-experienced the major traumatic or unresolved events
of her life that had occurred when she was at a particular weight.*
Thus her descent from two hundred fifty pounds set
her spinning backward in time through the emotionally
charged events of her life: leaving Texas for New York
(210 pounds), her college graduation (190 pounds), her
decision to drop the pre-med curriculum (and to give up

the dream of discovering the cure for the cancer that killed her father) (180 pounds), her loneliness at her high school graduation—her envy of other daughters and fathers, her inability to get a date for the senior prom (170 pounds), her junior high graduation and how much she missed her father at that graduation (155 pounds). What a wonderful proof of the unconscious realm! Betty's body had remembered what her mind had long forgotten.

Memories of her father permeated these flashbacks. The closer we looked, the more apparent it was that everything led back to him, to his death, and to the one hundred fifty pounds Betty weighed at that time. The closer she approached that weight, the more depressed she grew and the more her mind swarmed with feelings and recollections of her father.

Soon we spent entire sessions talking about her father. The time had come to unearth everything. I plunged her into reminiscence and encouraged her to express everything she could remember about his illness, his dying, his appearance in the hospital the last time she saw him, the details of his funeral, the clothes she wore, the minister's speech, the people who attended.

Betty and I had talked about her father before but never with such intensity and depth. She felt her loss as never before and, over a two-week period, wept almost continuously. We met thrice weekly during this time, and I attempted to help her understand the source of her tears. In part she cried because of her loss, but in large part because she considered her father's life to have been such a tragedy: he never obtained the education he wanted (or that she wanted for him), and he died just before he retired and never enjoyed the years of leisure for which he had longed. Yet, as I pointed out to her, her description of his life's activities—his large extended family, his wide social circle, his daily bull sessions with friends, his love of the land, his youth in the navy, his afternoons fishing—was a picture of a full life in which her father was immersed in a community of people who knew and loved him.

When I urged her to compare his life with her own, she realized that some of her grief was misplaced: it was her own life, not her father's, that was tragically unfulfilled. How much of her grief, then, was for all her unrealized hopes? This question was particularly painful for Betty who, by that time, had visited a gynecologist and been told that she had an endocrine disorder that would make it impossible for her to have children.

I felt cruel during these weeks because of the pain our therapy was uncovering. Every session was an ordeal, and Betty often left my office badly shaken. She began to have acute panic attacks and many disturbing dreams, and, as she put it, she died at least three times a night. She could not remember the dreams except for two recurrent ones that had begun in adolescence, shortly after her father's death. In one dream, she lay paralyzed in a small closet which was being bricked up. In the other, she was lying in a hospital bed with a candle, which represented her soul, burning at the head of the bed. She knew that when the flame went out she would die, and she felt helpless as she watched it get smaller and smaller.

Discussing her father's death obviously evoked fears of her own death. I asked Betty to talk about her first experiences and early conceptions of death. Living on a ranch, she was no stranger to death. She watched her mother kill chickens and heard the squeal of hogs being slaughtered. Betty was extremely unsettled by her grandfather's death when she was nine. According to her mother (Betty told me she had no recollection of this), she was reassured by her parents that only old people die, but then she pestered them for weeks by chanting she didn't want to grow old and by repeatedly asking her parents how old they were. But it was not until shortly after her father died that Betty grasped the truth about the inevitability of her own death. She remembered the precise moment.

"It was a couple days after the funeral, I was still taking off from school. The teacher said I should return when I felt ready. I could have gone back earlier, but it didn't seem right to go back so soon. I was worried that people wouldn't think I was sad enough. I was walking in the fields behind the house. It was cold out—I could see my breath, and it was hard to walk because the earth was clumped and the plow ridges were frozen. I was thinking of my father lying beneath the ground and how cold he must have been, and I suddenly heard a voice from above saying to me, 'You're next!' "

Betty stopped and looked at me. "You think I'm crazy?"

"No, I told you before, you don't have the knack for it."

She smiled. "I've never told that story to anyone. In fact I'd forgotten it, forgotten it for years until this week."

"I feel good you're willing to trust me with it. It sounds important. Say some more about being 'next.'"

"It's like my father was no longer there to protect me. In a way he stood between me and the grave. Without him there, I was next in line." Betty hunched up her shoulders and shuddered. "Can you believe I still feel spooky when I think about this?"

"Your mother? Where was she in all this?"

"Like I've told you before—way, way in the background. She cooked and she fed me—she was real good at that—but she was weak—I was the one protecting her. Can you believe a Texan who can't drive? I started driving at twelve when my father got sick, because she was afraid to learn."

"So there was no one shielding you?"

"That's when I started having nightmares. That dream about the candle—I must have had it twenty times."

"That dream makes me think of what you said before about your fear of losing weight, about having to stay heavy to avoid dying of cancer like your father. If the candle flame stays fat, you live."

"Maybe, but sounds farfetched."

Another good example, I thought, of the pointlessness of the therapist rushing in with an interpretation, even a good one like this. Patients, like everyone else, profit most from a truth they, themselves, discover.

Betty continued, "And somewhere in that year I got the idea I was going to die before I was thirty. You know, I think I still believe that."

These discussions undermined her denial of death. Betty began to feel unsafe. She was always on guard against injury—when driving, bicycling, crossing the street. She became preoccupied with the capriciousness of death. "It could come at any instant," she said, "when I least expect it." For years her father had saved money and planned a family trip to Europe only to develop a brain tumor shortly before the departure date. She, I, anyone, can be struck down at any time. How does anyone, how do *I*, cope with that thought?

Now committed to being entirely "present" with Betty, I tried not to flinch from any of her questions. I told her of my own difficulties in coming to terms with death; that, though the fact of death cannot be altered, one's attitude toward it can be vastly influenced. From both my personal and my professional experience, I have come to believe that the fear of death is always greatest in those who feel that they have not lived their life fully. A good working formula is: the more unlived life, or unrealized potential, the greater one's death anxiety.

My hunch was, I told Betty, that when she entered

more fully into life, she would lose her terror of death—some, not all of it. (We are all stuck with some anxiousness about death. It's the price of admission to self-awareness.)

At other times Betty expressed anger at my forcing her to think about morbid topics. "Why think about death? We can't do anything about it!" I tried to help her understand that, though the *fact* of death destroys us, the *idea* of death can save us. In other words, our awareness of death can throw a different perspective on life and incite us to re-arrange our priorities. Carlos had learned that lesson—it was what he meant on his deathbed when he talked about his life having been saved.

It seemed to me that an important lesson Betty could learn from an awareness of death was that life had to be lived *now;* it could not be indefinitely postponed. It was not difficult to lay out before her the ways she avoided life: her reluctance to engage others (because she dreaded separa-tion); her overeating and obesity, which had resulted in her being left out of so much life; her avoidance of the present moment by slipping quickly into the past or the future. It was also not difficult to argue that it was within her power to change these patterns—in fact she had already begun: consider how she was engaging me that very day!

I encouraged her to plunge into her grief; I wanted her to explore and express every facet of it. Again and again, I asked the same question: "Who, what, are you grieving for?"

Betty responded, "I think I'm grieving for love. My

daddy was the only man who ever held me in his arms. He was the only man, the only person, who told me he loved me. I'm not sure that will come my way again."

I knew we were entering an area where once I would never have dared to go. It was hard to remember that less than a year before it had been difficult for me even to look at Betty. Today I felt positively tender toward her. I stretched to find a way to respond, but still it was less than I wanted to give.

"Betty, being loved is not sheer chance or fate. You can influence it—more than you think. You are much more available for love now than you were a few months ago. I can see, I can feel the difference. You look better, you relate better, you are so much more approachable and available now."

Betty was more open with her positive feelings toward me and shared long daydreams in which she became a physician or a psychologist and she and I worked together side by side on a research project. Her wish that I could have been her father led us into one final aspect of her grief that had always caused her much torment. Alongside her love for her father, she also had negative feelings: she felt ashamed of him, of his appearance (he was extremely obese), of his lack of ambition and education, of his ignorance of social amenities. As she said this, Betty broke down and sobbed. It was so hard to talk about this, she said, because she was so ashamed of being ashamed of her own father.

As I searched for a reply, I remembered something my first analyst, Olive Smith, said to me over thirty years before. (I remember it well, I think, because it was the only remotely personal—and the most helpful—thing she said in my six hundred hours with her.) I had been badly shaken by having expressed some monstrous feelings about my mother, and Olive Smith leaned over the couch and said gently, "That just seems to be the way we're built."

I cherished those words; and now, thirty years later, I passed along the gift and said them to Betty. The decades had eroded none of their restorative powers: she exhaled deeply, calmed herself, and sat back in her chair. I added that I knew personally how difficult it is for highly educated adults to relate to uneducated blue-collar parents.

Betty's year-and-a-half assignment in California was now drawing to a close. She did not want to stop therapy and asked her company to extend her time in California. When that failed, she considered searching for a job in California but ultimately decided to return to New York.

What a time to stop—in the midst of work on important issues and with Betty still camped outside the one-hundred-fifty-pound roadblock! At first I thought that the timing could not have been worse. Yet, in a more reflective moment, I realized that Betty may have plunged so deeply into therapy *because of*, not despite, our limited time frame. There is a long tradition in psychotherapy going back to Carl Rogers and, before him, to Otto Rank, which understood that a pre-set termination date often increases the efficiency of therapy. Had Betty not known that her time in therapy was limited, she might, for example, have taken far longer to achieve the inner resolve she needed to begin her weight loss.

Besides, it was by no means clear that we could have gone much further. In our last months of therapy, Betty seemed interested more in resolving the issues we had already opened than in uncovering new ones. When I recommended that she continue therapy in New York and offered her the name of a suitable therapist, she was noncommittal, stating that she wasn't sure whether she would continue, that maybe she had done enough.

There were other signs as well that Betty might go no further. Though not bingeing, she was no longer dieting. We agreed to concentrate on maintaining her new weight of one hundred sixty and, to that end, Betty bought a whole new wardrobe.

A dream illuminated this juncture in therapy:

I dreamed that the painters were supposed to paint the outside trim on my house. They were soon all over the house. There was a man at every window with a spray gun. I got dressed quickly and tried to stop them. They were painting the whole outside of the house. There were wisps of smoke coming up all over the house from between the floorboards. I saw a painter with a stocking over his face spraying inside the house. I told him I just wanted the trim painted. He said he had orders to paint everything, inside and out. "What is the smoke?" I asked. He said

it was bacteria and added they had been in the kitchen cultur-
ing deadly bacteria. I got scared and kept saying over and over,
"I only wanted the trim painted."

At the onset of therapy, Betty had indeed wanted only
the trim painted but had been drawn inexorably into recon-
structive work on the deep interior of her house. Moreover, the painter-therapist had sprayed death—her father's
death, her own death—into her house. Now she was saying
she had gone far enough; it was time to stop.

As we neared our final session, I felt a mounting relief
and exhilaration—as though I had gotten away with something. One of the axioms of psychotherapy is that the
important feelings one has for another *always* get commu-
nicated through one channel or another—if not verbally,
then nonverbally. For as long as I can remember, I have
taught my students that if something big in a relationship is
not being talked about (by either patient or therapist), then
nothing else of importance will be discussed either.

Yet I had started therapy with intense negative feelings about Betty—feelings I had never discussed with her
and that she had never recognized. Nevertheless, without
doubt, we had discussed important issues. Without doubt,
we had made progress in therapy. Had I disproven the cat-
echism? Are there no "absolutes" in psychotherapy?

Our final three hours were devoted to work on Betty's
distress at our impending separation. What she had feared
at the very onset of treatment had come to pass: she had

allowed herself to feel deeply about me and was now going to lose me. What was the point of having trusted me at all? It was as she had said at first: "No involvement, no separation."

I was not dismayed by the re-emergence of these old feelings. First, as termination approaches, patients are bound to regress temporarily. (*There* is an absolute.) Second, issues are never resolved once and for all in therapy. Instead, therapist and patient inevitably return again and again to adjust and to reinforce the learning—indeed, for this very reason, psychotherapy has often been dubbed "cyclotherapy."

I attempted to address Betty's despair, and her belief that once she left me all our work would come to naught, by reminding her that her growth resided neither in me nor in any outside object, but was a part of her, a part she would take with her. If, for example, she was able to trust and to reveal herself to me more than to anyone previously, then she contained within herself that experience as well as the ability to do it again. To drive my point home, I attempted, in our final session, to use myself as an example.

"It's the same with me, Betty. I'll miss our meetings. But I'm changed as a result of knowing you—"

She had been crying, her eyes downcast, but at my words she stopped sobbing and looked toward me, expectantly.

"And, even though we won't meet again, I'll still retain that change."

"What change?"

"Well, as I mentioned to you, I hadn't had much professional experience with…er…with the problem of obesity—" I noted Betty's eyes drop with disappointment and silently berated myself for being so impersonal.

"Well, what I mean is that I hadn't worked before with heavy patients, and I've gotten a new appreciation for the problems of—" I could see from her expression that she was sinking even deeper into disappointment. "What I mean is that my attitude about obesity has changed a lot. When we started I personally didn't feel comfortable with obese people—"

In unusually feisty terms, Betty interrupted me. "Ho! ho! ho! 'Didn't feel comfortable'—that's putting it mildly. Do you know that for the first six months you hardly ever looked at me? And in a whole year and a half you've never—not once—touched me? Not even for a handshake!"

My heart sank. My God, she's right! I *have* never touched her. I simply hadn't realized it. And I guess I didn't look at her very often, either. I hadn't expected her to notice!

I stammered, "You know, psychiatrists don't ordinarily touch their—"

"Let me interrupt you before you tell any more fibs and your nose gets longer and longer like Pinocchio." Betty seemed amused at my squirming. "I'll give you a hint. Remember, I'm in the same group with Carlos and we often chat after the group about you."

Uh-oh, I knew I was cornered now. I hadn't anticipated this. Carlos, with his incurable cancer, was so isolated and felt so shunned that I had decided to support him by going out of my way to touch him. I shook his hand before and after each hour and usually put my hand on his shoulder as he left the office. Once, when he learned about the spread of his cancer to his brain, I held him in my arms while he wept.

I didn't know what to say. I couldn't point out to Betty that Carlos was a special case, that he needed it. God knows she had needed it, too. I felt myself flushing. I saw I had no choice but to own up.

"Well, you're pointing out one of my blind spots! It is true—or, rather, was true—that, when we first began to meet, I was put off by your body."

"I know. I know. It wasn't too subtle."

"Tell me, Betty, knowing this—seeing that I didn't look at you or was uncomfortable with you—why did you stay? Why didn't you stop seeing me and find someone else? Plenty of other shrinks around." (Nothing like a question to get off the hot seat!)

"Well, I can think of at least two reasons. First, remember that I'm used to it. It's not like I expect anything more. Everyone treats me that way. People hate my looks. No one *ever* touches me. That's why I was surprised, remember, when my hairdresser massaged my scalp. And, even though you wouldn't look at me, you at least seemed interested in what I had to say—no, no, that's not right—you were interested in what I *could* or *might* say if I stopped being so jolly. Actually, that was helpful. Also, you didn't fall asleep. That was an improvement on Dr. Farber."

"You said there were two reasons."

"The second reason is that I could understand how you felt. You and I are very much alike—in one way, at least. Remember when you were pushing me to go to Overeaters Anonymous? To meet other obese people—make some friends, get some dates?"

"Yeah, I remember. You said you hated groups."

"Well, that's true. I do hate groups. But it wasn't the whole truth. The *real* reason is that *I* can't stand fat people. They turn my stomach. I don't want to be seen with them. So how can I get down on you for feeling the same way?"

We were both on the edge of our chairs when the clock said we had to finish. Our exchange had taken my breath away, and I hated to end. I didn't want to stop seeing Betty. I wanted to keep on talking to her, to keep on knowing her.

We got up to leave, and I offered her my hand, both hands.

"Oh no! Oh no, I want a hug! That's the only way you can redeem yourself."

When we embraced, I was surprised to find that I could get my arms all the way around her.

Big Time

I made it self-destruct. My body. I destroyed it.

It takes work to get as fat as I was. Not a fat child, I had to start pushing the limits in my teenage years. I'm five feet ten inches and at my most ambitious I weighed nearly four hundred pounds.

I filled out most in my shoulders, my back. I was massive; sometimes I went sideways through a door if it was slightly narrow. I liked it. It was a presence, my girth, that split crowds even from fifteen feet away. I could be benign and friendly without getting walked on like most quiet people. The only drawback was with women.

Luckily, I'm black. And because I am, being fat wasn't the death of my sexual life. I was not quite middle class, but the pool of women I floated in as a teenager were working women: not nurses, but their assistants, secretarial trainees, cosmetologists, and food servers at the concession stands of Yankee Stadium.

In the U.S., if you're really heavy you're probably not well off. Cheap, unimaginably unhealthy food is plentiful from Jamaica, Queens, to the hills of West Virginia. In this setting even 250 pounds wasn't beyond the realm of attraction. At 275, I was with a single mother who was considerate, kind, and funny. These women didn't find me gorgeous, but in their lives other characteristics far overshadowed my fifty-inch waist. Loyalty, consideration, a job. I coasted on their woeful expectations for as long as I could, a chunky knight in shining stretch pants.

But then came college.

Five hours upstate, I discovered another continent, one that found my fat distasteful, even offensive. And it was black women as much as any others who rejected me. I was in the middle class, the women were self-sufficient, thus the size of my ass was as important as my personality. More.

Though I made friends, socialized, I often found myself marching spitefully through a dining hall, my tray loaded with donuts and imitation Philly cheesesteaks, as if I could hide from the collective grimaces and smirks in my rising pile of candied treats. You think I'm nasty, well watch this. That was my battle cry. The more my friends went to play basketball or jog or shotput, the more bags of

Doritos, jars of peanut butter and three-liter Pepsis I consumed. It was self-destruction, just not as sexy as cocaine
or alcohol. With liquor you become loose and loquacious,
but no one has ever turned charming after downing a
whole bucket of extra-crispy fried chicken.

It was a tantrum, but I enjoyed it. I like eating. When
I'd swallowed half a log of raw cookie dough and my
temples hurt, my stomach felt distended, near bursting, I
would peel off the rest of the wrapper and force myself to
eat the remains in front of a mirror in my dorm room. I
was watching myself, chastising myself, saying, "Okay, if
you're going to die like this, let's die."

The summer before my senior year of college I was
three hundred and fifty. I couldn't get a date, but I couldn't
be quite sure how unattractive I'd become. I was still
friendly, I made jokes, and, in my mind, if I saw a woman
smiling at me as she laughed I still had a chance.

I did not.

This became clear finally when one young woman and
I spent many days together in the summer of 1994. She
was slight and moved easily, always, as though she'd never
had to give her body a thought. At the end of the summer
she told my friend that I was "her perfect man, but he's big
enough to be two perfect men."

It was an alarm bell, but I ignored it. I decided that all
women were bitches and I returned to my dimly lit cave
with a bag of Slim Jims and a forty-ounce container of
Cool Whip.

My room did have a phone. A copy of the *Village Voice* sat on my bed. I flipped through the back pages, looking at the naked girls posed in the phone sex ads (there hadn't yet been the boom in "bodywork" ads). Beside these I found another number, half a page high. The ad read: meet real live women in your area who are horny and dying to meet you.

It worked.

I met some.

They were not prostitutes.

The women on the line lived in the Bronx or Brooklyn. Not all the women who ever called, but all the women I ever met.

The first time, I took a Shortline bus down to Manhattan from Ithaca, then a train back up to the South Bronx. I weaved through a cracked lobby door, then climbed to the second floor to meet a woman in her thirties who, based on two phone conversations, had assured me that if I wanted, she'd have my baby. I was up for the offer. Not the result of procreation, but the act that can result in it.

At her door I was aware of that eye that every man gets used to, the eye of a woman's appraisal. In this case, the once-over was done quickly and expertly, like a jeweler's, though willing to accept a great many more flaws.

She wasn't pretty, but she looked better than me. We sat on her couch in the living room of her two-room apartment. We talked, but she sat far back, like an interviewer.

Which she was. I lost my charm in front of her and she decided against a night of passion. She stood, went to her bedroom, unlocked the door and let out her son. He was about six and happy to play card games with his mother and me. Eventually I cobbled together enough indignation to leave. "I'm going," I said. She was on the phone. She said, "Yeah."

The next time I came down to New York City, I made sure to ask first, "Are we going to fuck?"

The woman said, "If you eat my pussy first."

I went to her apartment, also in the Bronx. She called herself Big Time. She was a grandmother and she was thirty-nine.

Big Time met me in front of her building wearing tight pants for the same reason I did: there was no such thing as baggy for men and women like us. She was pleasant. She was businesslike. I came into the apartment, she took me to the bedroom, pulled off her clothes, lay on the mattress, opened her legs, and then parted the lips of her vagina.

Meanwhile I stood there so dressed I hadn't even untied my shoelaces. She chided me. She got up to offer me a beer, but I don't drink beer so she gave me Courvoisier.

We got loose. I turned off the light and ate her pussy. Then I ate her ass. Later she jerked me off. I left without sleeping over.

It was like that every weekend I could put such an event together. It became expensive: calling to meet more women at fifty-five cents a minute, the cost of bus tickets.

But the payoff was pretty good. I very rarely had intercourse, but hand jobs and blow jobs, they work. And I enjoyed going down on the women. They weren't looking at me when I did that. Their eyes were closed. Pretty soon I was eating more pussy than a four-year lesbian.

What I found most surprising was that the women weren't as ashamed as I was. They never wanted to turn off the lights. If I brought up the idea they were flummoxed, as if I'd suggested moving to another neighborhood—the possibility didn't occur to them. In our couplings, I was the demure one.

I suppose this might be seen as liberating. I was with women for whom the conventions of beauty did not apply. Isn't that the grand free space so many of us wish for? We could be blissful in our size, together.

Except that they did, in fact, find me unappealing, and told me so. They let me know that they didn't usually like their men so "thick," that most often they liked burly, muscled figures. I apologized a lot.

But in my mind I ridiculed them. I thought they were too stupid to know they appeared wretched and tired, that they gave off the stale odor of perspiration and nacho chips. I thought of them as animals and of myself as less than an animal, because I was beholden to them, forced to endure their mind-numbingly loud conversation the way they endured my bloated, sagging body just to bust their nut.

And every woman wanted me out before dawn. There seemed to be a general agreement amongst them that I would never be allowed to spend the night. There was great shame in being rushed to collect one's clothes, ushered to the door, unceremoniously led out. I often felt they wanted me gone before their neighbors came out to see me lumber awkwardly down the hall. It was a dull, distant humiliation, but on the train back to my mother's house or the next day on the bus up to Ithaca, I assured myself that it had been a good time.

At school I discovered a great love for books. In my last year I did a lot of catching up. I don't make claims that I charted vast new intellectual territory, but I found myself very happy when I was reading, so I kept reading. Then I began to write.

I came back to New York to go to graduate school, but I didn't call that number. I was living at home with my family so I didn't want the phone bill coming in screaming "Fuck Line!" when my mother opened it.

More than that, I stopped wanting to go out. I didn't have energy to go bump uglies with anyone. Like a distance runner's coach, my mind was propelling me forward (go meet another one! another one!), but my body had given out. I grew fatigued at the sight of the green-line trains that ran service up to the Bronx. Instead I went to class. I went to work. I wrote.

I wrote a book.

After some disappointments we sold it. My agent nonchalantly reminded me there would be an author photo. She was only telling me so I'd reserve the time on my calendar, but I took it differently. *There would be a photo of me.* I went on a diet.

I am a creature of petty vanity, why lie? Living as an obtrusive, ungainly mess was one thing, but having it photographed, preserved, was another. I was pragmatic. I was a businessman. My publishing house would send me out to meet more people if they believed people would want to meet me. It was a calculation. It was also an excuse.

I wanted to lose the weight. When I stopped reveling in my self-loathing long enough to contemplate my situation, I had to acknowledge that it was very hard to find clothes; I had a hard time finding seats to fit me; I was out of breath when I even thought about climbing a flight of stairs. I didn't like it anymore that people moved away from me before I'd ever met them. I was exhausted from being so large. I lost more than one hundred and fifty pounds.

A wonderful photographer took my picture. I looked good. The first time I saw it I cringed, but when I held my chest and stomach in mock humiliation there was less of me to clutch and that was nice. I thought, who better than me to try being handsome? Why not me?

At a writer's retreat in drab, dear Provincetown, Massachusetts, I met a woman. This was before the book came out, while I was editing it. She wrote fiction too. We became friends, then spent a few weeks flirting, going through town window shopping, trying not to spend our stipends too quickly. It was a milquetoast paradise. Get up and write or read. Go for a jog. Go for a walk together.

Come home to read. Talk with the other painters and writers. Talk with Portuguese fishermen and the aging transsexuals living on the beach. Go home to write. Then drink hooch. Wake up in the middle of the night to write down a line or idea, then while still up pour some Knob Creek in a small glass and read a bit more. Do this for seven months and be content.

I was more surprised than joyous when she wanted to kiss me. It happened late one evening when I stormed out of a bar as a joke and she followed. Her face was on my chest and my first reaction was to curl up so she couldn't feel my doughy folds, but many of them were gone. Not all, but plenty. She squeezed me like there would be nothing else she would ever want to do with my body, and I was very surprised.

While it's impossible to hide the learned movements of heavier years—hiding behind towels after showering, wearing a big coat even on warm days, not wearing short-sleeved shirts, no shorts, not even sandals—I consciously tried to stop those actions, to hide them away. I thought that if I acted like a slimmer person I would eventually believe I'd become one.

It worked to a degree, but like those anorexic girls in teen after-school specials, what I see in the mirror is still that weary, wider guy. My face seems puffy unless I catch it at a quick glance, before I have time to remember how it looked for so long. My body, even as my waist size plummets toward normal, never seems any more svelte. I have to touch myself with my eyes closed to feel how my stomach is flatter, how it sucks in when I lie on my back, though before it bubbled up, bubbled over. I touch my ass and it's like I'm copping a feel of someone else's. It's tight as a snare drum.

I thought for years that I simply couldn't get a date with a woman, that I had to resort to hurried, tussled fucking with someone who didn't care to know my name. But I chose that. I wanted to be treated like I felt. And they wanted to treat someone that way. That feeling has gone for me. Or at least now when it surfaces I quickly set down to write some vile little story and get it out that way.

Only occasionally do I fantasize this plan: to run and diet and sculpt some very nice shape for myself, taking three more years to do it, until my body is as perfect as it's going to be, then swallow a grenade and send the whole damn thing to hell.

Very often my girlfriend, the author from Provincetown, tells me she finds me handsome. She loves me so I imagine she can't say anything else. I take her words as kindness. But I don't want to act as though I have only one face and it's a mopey one. I have many. One day I feel like I've actually put on weight, like I'm six hundred pounds and this new life is the last choked dream of my heart being crushed. But then the next day I go out and am sure there isn't a motherfucker on two feet who's sexier. On the good days I pose for my girl like I'm Steve Reeves from the old Hercules movies. And on the really good days I mean it.

STEPHEN KUUSISTO

Fatland

There was a time in my life when for compli-
cated reasons I became quite fat. I say "quite fat" because I
wish to distinguish my fatness from the merely pudgy or
flabby. The latter denote quiet excess: lingering at tables
long after supper with the bleu cheese and dessert wines.
Mine was what you might call a ravening fatness. I was the
fat thing inside the moon.

No one who visits that country ever forgets it. Having
reverted to a leaner state, come down from the mountain
so to speak, I still squeeze into taxicabs and feel the old
ghost.

"My face," Auden once wrote, "looks like a wedding-
cake left out in the rain." This is fine. But a fat man's face
is a superior ruin, a vault filled with unthinkable life.

Monkeys dance here. O thousands of appetites are on the
loose!

It began in 1968. Until then I'd been a skinny child. But
now I was thirteen and neurasthenic and blind and lonely
and I daily faced children in school who called me "blindo"
or "Magoo." They spoke of me in the third person: I was
the "it"—a kid with a disability in public space. And then it
happened—the thing Freud calls "the incitement"—the
moment when personality trips a switch. I decided to become a fat person.

I remember the moment perfectly.

I was barely home from school. My shirt was torn
where a tall and oddly stinky boy named Jerry had ripped
the shoulder seam of my button-down shirt while shouting
wildly, "Let's court-martial him! Let's brand him for being a
deserter! He's a traitor to our country!"

With that, five boys from the sixth grade piled on top
of me. I'd been sitting alone under a birch tree listening to
the red-winged blackbirds, which sometimes sounded like
pocket combs scraped by a thumbnail. In other words, I
was doing what blind kids did—I was sitting alone at recess
and listening to the delicate engines of the insects.

Now Jerry and the boys were holding me down in the
grass, punching my arms, tearing my sleeves, singing a television sitcom theme song that had something to do with
branding a man who was a traitor to the Union army. My

thick glasses flew away into the underbrush. My thin spine buckled. My face went deep into the wild rhubarb leaf and dead leaves.

They sang on top of me in unison, like the Hitler youth.

> *What do you do when you're branded*
> *And you know you're a man?*

"Aw shit," said Jerry, "he's too skinny for branding!" They took to punching each other and then they ran away in a kind of scrum, slapping each other and laughing as they disappeared.

At home I opened a can of Swedish meatballs and ate them with my fingers. They were gelatinous and cold and were indistinguishable from dog food.

I switched on the television and caught the middle of the *Four O'Clock Movie*—*The Great Caruso* starring Mario Lanza as the noble and fat Italian tenor.

Caruso unrolls onto the stage: immense, elegant, wearing laurels in a cone of light.

I decide I shall be big.

I can smell Jerry's sweat on my torn sleeve, odor of apples and methane.

I will be big!

In this pursuit I was aided by the television. Though I could not see the pictures on the screen I could hear that Detroit was burning and Watts was burning and even the

Cuyahoga River was burning. I leaned close to the screen and chewed in my prismatic solitude.

Becoming fat by design differs from involuntary obesity.

One may feel sorry for the hopelessly fat children on television programs—Maury Povich parades before a live studio audience a dozen two-hundred-pound toddlers wearing only their colossal diapers and dim-witted smiles. These are the freaks. Pitiable. Unknowing. Sodden in their blubber. Scarcely able to walk...

Ah, but the designed fat man or child is the emperor. A fat boy who has chosen his craft is a prince! He covers the dark emptiness with his wide face. It is the only language in which you don't open your lips. You stand. You are a lighthouse. Falstaff with his lantern...

I am growing bigger.

I cannot play sports because of my blindness.

I am invited nowhere and my mother, who is alcoholic, who sleeps all afternoon, my horror show mother, has filled the house with rich and fattening foods.

When I eat I am like a mirror facing a mirror. There is no other place.

Eating is the electrolysis of mystical and eternal love.

I am growing.

I eat astonishing things in my effort to become transformed.

I eat lychee nuts from a can, letting them wander over my tongue and palate.

I eat a mango with the aid of a spray can of whipped cream.

I eat Swedish crackers that taste like pinecones.

I eat an entire chunk of Gorgonzola cheese.

By day I am the blind kid who stands in the tall grass while the others play ball. In the school yard I squint in my privacy and practice Latin declensions while boys scream and baseballs are hit in the crisp air.

But now with my amazing sticky hands I am my own maker.

I am eating in a Jungian fashion, eating for the pleasure of my subconscious selves. The bookish blind kid who is determined to become fat has his own green Eleusinian grove.

I eat cold lobster, dipping morsels in hot butter.

I fry a steak and smother it in cheddar cheese.

I bake my own pies: cherry, apple, rhubarb...

I bathe sliced mushrooms in butter and fry them with bacon and thinly sliced liver.

I taste maple syrup from a can.

While my teenage friends argue over which of the Beatles is the best musician I study my own fat heroes.

In effect I am building a pantheon of the "Great Fat."

Of course I start with Caruso the tenor who stood only a little over five feet and weighed almost three hundred pounds.

Then I discover Orson Welles, who ate fourteen trays of shrimp toast at Harry's Bar in Venice....

There's Buddha on his long, pure, beautiful road....

I discover John Adams, the second president of the United States: a brave and very fat man....

I am in love with the idea of stature.

I want to stand in the autumn sunlight wearing an elegant, dark suit and a wide brimmed hat.

In the school yard I'm a skinny, blind outcast.

At home I am transforming myself into Winston Churchill.

Soon my father is referring to me as "Uncle Vanya" owing to my new portliness and my penchant for wearing dark, three-piece suits. I even sport a gold pocket watch complete with chain and fob. I am a petty burgher from Cologne, a seller of hair tonics or meerschaum pipes.

My father is a thin man who is devoted to the art of personal denial. He was raised during the Great Depression by Scandinavian Lutheran parents. Worse yet, his father was a minister. My father grew up quite literally by eating on the barter system. Parishioners paid their minister with chickens and potatoes. After a day presiding over funerals my father's family ate the simple food of gratitude. Now his own son is eating to excess and dressing like a member of the Odd Fellows' Temple.

My efforts at bulking up are paying off! My somber and penurious father has noticed my new figure and he is shocked! He squints as if he's at the beach or some other horrible place.

"You are fat! My god! You look like a magpie!"

"I am not fat, I am merely cutting a figure!" I am seated before an enormous Dagwood sandwich.

"You are a fatty!" my father cries and wags his index finger. "You are a fatty and you look like an overstuffed bird!"

"I am going to be a man of consequence, like Rudyard Kipling!" I say, waving a steep wedge of sandwich. I don't really remember whether Kipling is in the pantheon of fat heroes or not, but it slips out and sounds good.

"Bah!" says my father. He is one of the few persons I've ever met who actually says "Bah!"

"Bah! You are a magpie!"

I am very pleased.

My father is a workaholic. He's a university administrator. The nation is burning. He is preoccupied and he's scarcely at home. But now he has noticed that I look like a petty burgher from Austria. I am something other than the blind kid standing alone in the tall grass.

Later that night I hear my parents fighting over my new size. My mother has had plenty to drink and my father has most certainly endeavored to keep up with her. Like all drunk people they are too loud. I can hear them without leaving my room.

"Look what you've gone and done!" my father shouts. "You've turned him into a fatty!"

"I've done no such thing," says my mother with the dignified firmness of Irish drinkers. "He's studying to be a chef!"

It's the perfect thing to say. My father has no place in his mental Rolodex for the idea that his son might become a chef. In fact my father is intimidated by sit-down restaurants and avoids them.

"A chef!" he sniffs. "A chef!"

Out in the world I matter in an odd, new way. The playground boys who bullied me when I was just a blind kid are now interested in me—it's as if I'm missing a thumb on one hand. Where blindness is vaguely frightening to the boys, fatness is "real." We discourse on the advantages and disadvantages of foodstuffs. And I regale them with tales of Babe Ruth's appetite, telling them how the Yankee slugger ate a dozen hot dogs between innings of a game.

Jerry, my old nemesis, wants to know if today's players eat as much as the old guys.

"Well, Jerry," I say knowingly, "Mickey Mantle and Whitey Ford drink Jack Daniel's and ginger ale at Sardi's until they can barely speak. Then they each eat an eighteen-ounce porterhouse with mushrooms."

"How do you know that?" Jerry asks.

"Trust me," I say.

And he does.

I'm large.

In a certain way I will always be large.

I suppose that fatness taught me how to stand in a group; how to hold still; how to let people come to me. My sojourn in fatland lasted from 1968 until 1972. My beautiful fatness was an escape from basement sorrows: It brought me out into public places with a kind of gentleman's dignity.

My metabolism would ultimately not sustain obesity and I found that I was only a tourist in the world of the fat. But I remember its appetites and its flowers of status.

Hunger

This is the story of how, at the age of thirty-three, I learned to feed myself.

To begin with, here's what I did until then: I ate, starved, binged, purged, grew fat, grew thin, grew fat, grew thin, binged, purged, dieted, was good, was bad, grew fat, grew thin, grew thinner.

I had been a lean and energetic girl, always hungry, always eating, always thin. But I weighed 100 pounds at thirteen, 130 at fourteen. For the next ten years, I dieted. It is a long, dull story. I had lots of secrets and worries about me and food and my body. It was very scary and obsessive, the way it must feel for someone who is secretly and entirely illiterate.

One week after my father was diagnosed with brain cancer, I discovered bulimia. I felt like I'd discovered the secret to life, because you could eat yourself into a state of emotional numbness but not gain weight. Then I learned how to do it more effectively by reading articles in women's magazines on how to stop doing it. I barfed, but preferred laxatives. It was heaven: I lost weight.

All right, OK: there were some problems. I was scared all the time, full of self-loathing, and my heart got funky. When you've lost too much water and electrolytes, your muscular heart cramps up; it races like a sewing machine. Sometimes it would skip beats, and other times there would be a terrible feeling of vacuum, as if there were an Alhambra water tank in my heart and a big bubble had just burbled to the surface.

I would try to be good, in the puritanical sense, which meant denying my appetites. Resisting temptation meant I was good—strong, counter-animal—and I'd manage to re-sist fattening foods for a while. But then the jungle drums would start beating again.

I looked fine on the outside: thin, cheerful, even suc-cessful. But on the inside, I was utterly obsessed. I went into a long and deep depression after seeing some photos of people on a commune, working with their hands and primitive tools and workhorses, raising healthy food. I could see that they were really tuned to nature, to the sea-sons, to a direct sense of bounty, where you plant some-thing and it grows and you cut it down or pick it and eat it, savoring it and filling up on it. But I was a spy in the world of happy eating, always hungry, or stuffed, but never full.

Luckily I was still drinking at the time.

But then all of a sudden I wasn't. When I quit in 1986, I started getting healthier in almost every way and I had all these women helping me, and I told them almost every crime and secret I had, because I believed them when they said that we are as sick as our secrets. My life got much sweeter right away, and less dramatic; the pond inside me began to settle, and I could see through the water, which was the strangest sensation because for all those years I'd been taking various sticks—desperate men, financial drama, impossible deadlines—and stirring that pond water up. So now I was noticing beautiful little fish and dreamy underwater plants, and shells lying in the sand. I started getting along with myself pretty well for the first time in my life. But I couldn't or wouldn't tell anyone that for the last ten years I had been bingeing and purging, being on a diet, being good, getting thin, being bad, getting fat.

I remember hanging out with these people, letting their stories wash over me, when all of a sudden the thing inside would tap me on the shoulder and whisper, "OK, honey, let's go." And I'd cry out inwardly, No! No! "Sorry," it would say, "time to go shopping." And silently I'd cry out, Please don't make me go shopping! I'm not even hungry! "Shh, shh," it would whisper. "Let's go."

I felt that when I got sober, God had saved me from drowning, but now I was going to get kicked to death on the beach. It's so much hipper to be a drunk than a bulimic. Drunks are like bikers or wrestlers; bulimics are baton twirlers, gymnasts. The voice would say how sorry it was, but then glance down at its watch, tap its foot and sigh, and I'd sigh loudly too, and get up, and trudge behind it to the store.

It was actually more painful than that. It reminded me of the scene in Kazantzakis's *The Last Temptation of Christ*, when Jesus is walking along in the desert, really wanting to spend his life in a monastery praying, secluded and alone with God. Only of course God has different plans for him and, to get his attention, sends eagles down to wrap their talons around Jesus' heart, gripping him so that he falls to the sand in pain.

I did not feel eagle talons, but I felt gripped in the heart by a presence directing me to do exactly what it said. It said it was hungry and we had to go to the store.

So that voice and I would go buy the bad things—the chocolates, the Cheetos, the Mexican food—and big boxes of Epsom salts and laxatives. I grew weaker and more desperate until finally, one day in 1987, I called a woman named Rita Groszmann, who was listed in the Yellow Pages as a specialist in eating disorders. I told her what was going on and that I had no money, and she said to come in anyway, because she was afraid I was going to die. So I went in the next day.

I sat in her office and explained how I'd gotten started and that I wasn't ready to stop but that I was getting ready to be ready to stop. She said that was fine. I said that in fact I was going to go home that very night and eat chocolates and Mexican food and then purge. She said fine. I said, "Don't try to stop me." She said, "OK." I said, "There's nothing you can do to stop me, it's just the way it is," and we did this for half an hour or so, until she finally said very gently that she was not going to try to take my bulimia away from me. That she in fact was never going to take anything away from me, because I would try to get it back. But she said that I had some choices.

They were ridiculous choices. She proposed some, and I thought, This is the angriest person I've ever met. I'll give you a couple of examples. If I was feeling lonely and overwhelmed and about to binge, she said I could call someone up and ask them if they wanted to meet me for a movie. "Yeah," I said, "right." Or here's another good one: If I was feeling very *other*, sad and scared and overwhelmed, I could invite someone over for a meal, and then see if he or she felt like going for a walk. It is only because I was raised to be Politeness Person that I did not laugh at her. It was like someone detoxing off heroin, who's itching to shoot up, being told to take up macramé.

She asked if I was willing to make one phone call after I ate and buy time. I could always purge if I needed to, but she wanted me to try calling one person and see what happened. Now I'm not stupid. I knew she was up to something.

But I was really scared by the power the bad voice had over me, and I felt beaten up and out of control, scared of how sick I had somehow become, how often my pulse raced and my heart skipped beats, scared that one time when the eagle talons descended, they would grip too hard and pop me open. So I agreed. I got home, ate a more or less regular meal, called a friend, made contact, and didn't purge. The next day, I ate a light breakfast and lunch, and then a huge dinner, rooting around the fridge and cupboards like a truffle pig. But then I called my younger brother. He came over. We went for a walk.

Several weeks later, during one of our sessions, Rita asked me what I'd had for breakfast. "Cereal," I said.

"And were you hungry when you ate?"

"What do you mean?" I asked.

"I mean, did you experience hunger, and then make breakfast?"

"I don't really understand what you're asking," I said.

"Let me put it this way," she said. "Why did you have breakfast?"

"Oh! I see," I said, "I had breakfast because it was breakfast time."

"But were you hungry?"

I stared at her a moment. "Is this a trick question?" I asked.

"No," she said. "I just want to know how you know it's time to eat."

"I know it's time to eat because it's mealtime," I said. "It's morning, so I eat breakfast, or it's midday, so I eat lunch. And so on."

To make a long story ever so slightly shorter, she finally

asked me what it felt like when I was hungry, and I could not answer. I asked her to explain what it felt like when she was hungry, and she described a sensation in her stomach of emptiness, an awareness of appetite.

So for the next week, my assignment was to notice what it felt like when I was hungry. It was so strange. I was once again the world's oldest toddler. I walked around peering down as if to look inside my stomach, as if it was one of those old-fashioned front-loading washing machines with a window through which you could see the soapy water swirling over your clothes. And I paid attention until I was able to isolate this feeling in my stomach, a gritchy kind of emptiness, like a rat was scratching at the door, wanting to be let in.

"Wonderful," Rita said, and then gave me my next assignment: first, to notice when I was hungry, and then— this blew my mind—to feed myself.

I practiced, and all of a sudden I was Helen Keller after she breaks the code for "water," walking around touching things, learning their names. Only in my case, I was discovering which foods I was hungry for, and what it was like to eat them. I felt a strange loneliness at first, but then came upon a great line in one of Geneen Roth's books on eating, which said that awareness was about learning to keep yourself company. So I'd feel the scratchy emptiness in my belly, and I'd mention to myself that I seemed hungry. And then I'd ask myself, in a deeply maternal way, what I felt like eating.

"Well, actually, I feel like some Cheetos," I might say. So I'd go and buy a bag of Cheetos, put some in a bowl, and eat them. God! It was amazing. Then I'd check in with myself: "Do you want some more?" I'd ask.

"No," I'd say. "But don't throw them out."

I had been throwing food out or wetting it in the sink since I was fourteen, ever since my first diet. Every time I broke down and ate forbidden foods, I would throw out or wet what I'd left uneaten, because each time I was about to start over and be good again.

"I'm hungry," I'd say to myself. "I'd like some frosting."

"OK."

"And some Cheetos."

So I'd have some frosting and some Cheetos for breakfast. I'd eat for a while. Then I'd check in with myself, kindly: "More?"

"Not now," I'd say. "But don't wet them. I might want some more later."

I ate frosting and Cheetos for weeks. Also, cookies that a local bakery made with M&M's instead of chocolate chips. I'd buy half a dozen and keep them on the kitchen counter. It was terrifying; it was like knowing there were snakes in my kitchen. I'd eat a little, stop when I was no longer hungry. "Want one more cookie?" I'd ask.

"No, thanks," I'd say. "But maybe later. Don't wet them."

I never wet another bag of cookies. One day I woke up

and discovered that I also felt like having some oranges, then rice, then sautéed bell peppers. Maybe also some days the random pound of M&M's. But from then on I was always able at least to keep whatever I ate down—or rather, in my case, up. I went from feeling like a Diane Arbus character, viewed through the lens of her self-contempt, to someone filmed by a friendly cousin, someone who gently noted the concentration on my face as I washed a colander of tiny new potatoes.

Over the years, my body has not gotten firmer. Just the opposite in fact. But when I feel fattest and flabbiest and most repulsive, I try to remember that gravity speaks; also, that no one needs that plastic-body perfection from women of age and substance. Also, that I do not live in my thighs or in my droopy butt. I live in joy and motion and cover-ups. I live in the nourishment of food and the sun and the warmth of the people who love me.

It is, finally, so wonderful to have learned to eat, to taste and love what slips down my throat, padding me, filling me up, that I'm not uncomfortable calling it a small miracle. A friend who does not believe in God says, "Maybe not a miracle, but a little improvement," but to that I say, Listen! You must not have heard me right: I couldn't *feed* myself! So thanks for your input, but I know where I was, and I know where I am now, and you just can't get here from there. Something happened that I had despaired would never happen. It was like being a woman who has despaired of ever getting to be a mother but who now cradles a baby. So it was either a miracle—Picasso said, "Everything is a miracle; it's a miracle that one does not dissolve in one's bath like a lump of sugar"—or maybe it was more of a gift, one that required some assembly. But whatever it was, learning to eat was about learning to live—and deciding to live; and it is one of the most radical things I've ever done.

A Shiner Like a Diamond

I'd been living in Manhattan for eight years when my father called, excited by the news that my sister Amy was scheduled to appear in a magazine article devoted to the subject of interesting New York women.

"Can you imagine?" he asked. "My God, put a camera in front of that girl, and she'll shine like a diamond! Between the single men and the job opportunities, her phone is going to be ringing right off the hook!" He paused for a moment, perhaps imagining the life of a young New York woman whose phone rings off the hook. "We just have to make sure that none of the wrong people call her. You'll take care of that, right?"

"I'm putting it on my to-do list as we speak."

"Good boy," he said. "The trouble is that she's just so

darn pretty. That's the danger right there. Plus, you know, she's a girl."

My father has always placed a great deal of importance on his daughters' physical beauty. It is, to him, their greatest asset, and he monitors their appearance with the intensity of a pimp. What can I say? He was born a long time ago and is convinced that marriage is a woman's only real shot at happiness. Because it was always assumed that we would lead professional lives, my brother and I were free to grow as plump and ugly as we liked. Our bodies were viewed as mere vehicles, pasty, potbellied machines designed to transport our thoughts from one place to another. I might wander freely through the house drinking pancake batter from a plastic bucket, but the moment one of my sisters overspilled her bikini, my father was right there to mix his metaphors. "Jesus, Flossie, what are we running here, a dairy farm? Look at you, you're the size of a house. Two more pounds, and you won't be able to cross state lines without a trucking license."

"Oh, Lou," my mother would moan, "for Christ's sake, give it a rest."

"Aw, baloney. They'll thank me for this later." He honestly thought he was doing his girls a favor, and it confused him when the thanks never came.

In response to his vigilance and pressure, my sisters grew increasingly defensive and self-conscious. The sole exception turned out to be Amy, who is capable of getting even without first getting mad. Nothing seems to stick to her, partly because she's so rarely herself. Her fondness for transformation began at an early age and has developed into something closely resembling a multiple personality disorder. She's Sybil with a better sense of humor, Eve without the crying jags. "And who are we today?" my mother used to ask, leading to Amy's "Who don't you want me to be?"

At the age of ten Amy was caught taking a fistful of twenties from an unguarded till at the grocery store. I was with her and marveled at my sister's deftness and complete lack of fear. When the manager was called, she calmly explained that she wasn't stealing, she was simply pretending to be a thief. "And thieves steal," she said. "So that's what I was doing." It all made perfect sense to her.

She failed first grade by pretending to be stupid, but the setback didn't seem to bother her. For Amy school was devoted solely to the study of her teachers. She meticulously charted the repetition of their shoes and earrings and was quick to pinpoint their mannerisms. After school, alone in her simulated classroom, she would talk like them, dress like them, and assign herself homework she would never complete.

She became a Girl Scout only to become her Girl Scout leader. For Christmases and birthdays she requested wigs and makeup, hospital gowns and uniforms. Amy became my mother, and then my mother's friends. She was great as Sooze Grossman and Eleanor Kelliher, but her best impersonation was of Penny Midland, a stylish fifty-year-old woman who worked part-time at an art gallery my parents visited on a regular basis. Penny's voice was deep and roughly textured. She wasn't shy, but when she spoke, certain words tended to leave her mouth reluctantly, as if they'd been forced out against their will.

Dressed in a caftan and an appropriate white pageboy wig, Amy began phoning my father at the office. "Lou Sedaris! Penny Midland here. How the...hell are you?"

Surprised that this woman would be calling him at work, our father feigned enthusiasm as best he could. "Penny! Well, what do you know. Gosh, it's good to hear your voice."

The first few times she called, Amy discussed gallery business but, little by little, began complaining about her husband, a Westinghouse executive named Van. There were problems at home. Her marriage, it seemed, was on the rocks.

Our father offered comfort with his standard noncommittal phrases, reminding Penny that there were two sides to every coin and that it's always darkest before the dawn.

"Oh, Lou. It just feels so good to...talk to someone who really...understands."

I walked into the kitchen late one afternoon and came upon my twelve-year-old sister propositioning our father with lines she'd collected from *Guiding Light*. "I think we've both seen this coming for a long...time. The only question left is…what are we going to do about it? Oh, baby, let's run wild."

This is what my mother meant when she accused people of playing a dangerous game. Were our father to accept Penny's offer, Amy would have known him as a philanderer and wondered who else he might have slept with. Everything he'd ever said would be shaded by doubt and called into question. Was that *really* a business trip, or had he snuck off to Myrtle Beach with one of the Strivides twins? Who *was* this man?

Amy studied her reflection in the oven door, arranging her white bangs and liking what she saw. "All I'm saying is that I find you to be a very attractive…man. Is that such…a crime?"

It is to his credit that our father was such a gentleman. Stammering that he was very flattered to be asked, he let Penny down as gently as possible. After offering to set her up with some available bachelors from his office and country club, he told my sister to take care of herself, adding that she was a very special woman who deserved to be happy.

It was years before Amy finally admitted what she had done. They were relatively uneventful years for our family but, I imagine, a very confusing period of time for poor Penny Midland, who was frequently visited at the art gallery by my father and any number of his divorced associates. "Here's the gal I was telling you about," he'd say. "Why don't I just take a look around and give you two a chance to talk."

The passage of time has not altered my father's obsessive attention to my sisters' weight and appearance. He wonders why the girls don't drop by more often, and then when they do, he opens the door asking, "Is it just my imagination, or have you put on a few pounds?"

Because she has maintained her beautiful skin and enviable figure, Amy remains my father's greatest treasure. She is by far the most attractive member of the family, yet she spends most of her time and money disguising herself beneath prosthetic humps and appliquéd skin diseases. She's got more neck braces and false teeth than she knows what to do with, and her drawers and closets overflow with human hair. Having dreamt of one for years, she finally broke down and bought half of a padded, custom-made "fatty suit," which she enjoys wearing beneath dirty sweatpants as tight and uninviting as sausage casings. Unable to afford the suit's matching top, she's been reduced to waddling the streets much like two women fused together in some sort of cruel experiment. From the waist up she's slim and fit, chugging forward on legs the size of tree trunks and followed by a wide, dimpled bottom so thick that she could sit on a knitting needle and never feel a thing.

She wore the fatty suit home one Christmas, and our father met us at the Raleigh airport. Visibly shaken, he managed to say nothing on the short ride to the house, but the moment Amy stepped into the bathroom he turned to me, shouting, "What the hell happened to her? Christ almighty, this is killing me! I'm in real pain here."

"What?"

"Your sister, that's what. I just saw her six months ago, and now the girl's the size of a tank! I thought you were supposed to be keeping an eye on her."

I begged him to lower his voice. "Please, Dad, don't mention it in front of her. Amy's very sensitive about her…you know."

"Her what? Go ahead and say it: *her big, fat ass.* That's what she's ashamed of, and she should be! You could land a chopper on an ass like that."

"Oh, Dad."

"Don't try to defend her, wiseguy. She's a single woman, and the clock is ticking away. Who's going to love her, who's going to marry her with an ass like that?"

"Well," I said, "from what I've been told, a lot of men *prefer* rear ends like that."

He looked at me with great pity, his heart breaking for the second time that day. "Man, what you don't know could fill a book."

My father composed himself when Amy reentered the room, but when she turned to open the refrigerator door, he acted as though she were tossing a lit match into the gas tank of his Porsche. "What in God's name are you doing? Look at you—you're killing yourself."

Amy stuck a tablespoon into an economy-size vat of mayonnaise.

"Your problem is that you're bored," my father said. "You're bored and lonely and you're eating garbage to fill the void. I know what you're going through, but believe me, you can beat this."

Amy denied that she was bored and lonely. The problem, she said, was that she was hungry. "All I had on the plane were a couple of Danish. Can we go out for pancakes?"

She kept it up until our father, his voice cracking with pain, offered to find her some professional help. He mentioned camps and personal trainers, offering to loan—no, give—her the money, "And on top of that, I'll pay you for every pound you take off."

When Amy rejected his offer, he attempted to set an example. His Christmas dinner was gone in three bites, and dessert was skipped in favor of a brisk two-mile run. "Anyone want to join me? Amy?" He extended his age-old exercise regimen from ten minutes to an hour and trotted in place while speaking on the telephone.

Amy kept to her fatty suit until her legs were chafed and pimpled. It was on the morning of our return flight that she finally revealed her joke, and our father wept with relief. "Ha-ha, you really had me going. I should have known you'd never do that to yourself. And it's really fake? Ha-ha."

He reflected upon the fatty suit for the next several months. "She had me fooled for a minute there, but even with a big, fat ass she can't disguise the fact that she's a beautiful person, both inside and out, and that's what really matters." His epiphany was short-lived, and as the photo shoot approached, he began calling me with technical questions. "Do you happen to know if this magazine will be hiring a professional beautician? I sure as hell hope so, because her hair is getting awfully thin. And what are they going to do about lighting? Can we trust the photographer to do a first-class job, or should we call and see if they can't come up with someone better?"

There's a lot I don't tell my father when he calls asking after Amy. He wouldn't understand that she has no interest in getting married and was, in fact, quite happy to break up with her live-in boyfriend, whom she replaced with an imaginary boyfriend named Ricky.

The last time she was asked out by a successful bachelor, Amy hesitated before saying, "Thanks for asking, but I'm really not into white guys right now."

That alone would have stopped my father's heartbeat. "The clock is ticking," he says. "If she waits much longer, she'll be alone for the rest of her life."

This appears to suit Amy just fine.

When my father phoned asking about the photo shoot, I pretended to know nothing. I didn't tell him that, at the scheduled time, my sister arrived at the studio with un-washed hair and took a seat beside the dozen other New York women selected by the magazine. She complimented them on their flattering, carefully chosen outfits and waited as they had their hair fashioned, their eyebrows trained, and their slight imperfections masked by powder.

When it was her turn at the styling table, Amy said, "I want to look like someone has beaten the shit out of me."

The makeup artist did a fine job. The black eyes and purple jaw were accentuated by an arrangement of scratch marks on her forehead. Pus-yellow pools girdled her scabbed nose, and her swollen lips were fenced with mean rows of brackish stitches.

Amy adored both the new look and the new person it allowed her to be. Following the photo shoot, she wore her bruises to the dry cleaner and the grocery store. Most people nervously looked away, but on the rare occasions someone would ask what happened, my sister would smile as brightly as possible, saying, "I'm in love. Can you believe it? I'm finally, totally in love, and I feel great."

Out of Habit,
I Start Apologizing

I am lying, facedown, on a massage table at the
Doral Hotel and Spa in Telluride, Colorado. I am here under false pretenses, a guest of the Doral and all its services,
because the manager hopes I will write a rave article about
the hotel. Because of his generosity, I am having several
things that I cannot even pronounce done to my body for
free. I've been bathed, oiled, rolfed, fangoed, facialed, shi-
atsued, reflexologized, stretched, pressed, and dried. More
people have seen my naked body in the last three days than
in the last three years, and I'm starting to get used to it, my
modesty slipping away. I've begun to float from personal
service room to personal service room in a fragrant, supple
semiconsciousness. So far I've lost three hotel bathrobes,
two sweatshirts, and my watch.

It is unlike me to have so much attention paid to my body, to pamper and indulge this fleshy mass that I have spent my whole life trying to reduce, or reshape, or disguise.

I'm being worked on, this hour, by a technician whose nametag says "Wendy," and she's doing something to me called the Rosen method, a loose combination of body massage and psychotherapy. Considering the fact that every insecurity I have ever harbored has had to do with the shape of my body, the Rosen method seems like the ideal treatment for me.

"You have such strong legs," Wendy says, "but you are using them to hold up the rest of your body, and that's not what they are for."

My legs are strong and beautiful; dancer's legs, my mother's legs: she spent a lifetime developing sinewy, shapely leg muscles, and then gave them, like a promise, to me.

"You are pulling your body up with your shoulders," Wendy says, "pushing and pulling, when you should only be supporting; no wonder everything is too tight."

I try to imagine standing without legs, or staying erect without shoulders, but quickly give up. I am already fanta-sizing about next hour's foot massage when Wendy says, "Is there some good reason you've convinced the rest of your body that your hips and stomach and pelvis don't even exist?"

When I was younger, I used to believe that if I were really thin I would be happy, and there is a part of me that still believes it's true. For a good part of my life I would have quite literally given anything to be thin…a finger, three toes, the sight in one eye. Now I find it only mildly surprising that for the majority of my lifetime I would have traded being pretty, whole, and fat for being ugly, deformed, and thin.

I am boating the whitewater section of the upper Dolores River at flood stage. With me in my sixteen-foot inflatable raft are three beautiful Texan women who literally can't fathom my strength. We are approaching an obstacle in the river known simply as the Wall, a place where almost the entire volume of water rushes into a huge sandstone monolith, dives under it, skims along its base, and comes out, frothy and white, on the other side.

Sneaking around the wall without hitting it requires lots of anticipation and, at this high river level, almost superhuman strength. A hundred yards downriver from me I see my husband's boat careen closer and closer to the wall; I see one of his passengers disappear under the lip of the boat's front tube, the other two dive behind him into the river's swirl. When his boat makes contact with the sandstone I hear the splintering of wood, see an oar fly high into the air, taste the sudden rush of adrenaline in the back of my mouth.

My husband is the strongest human being I know, but I have the advantage of being second. I pull on the oars harder than I've ever pulled before, completely alert, making every stroke count. A voice that I recognize as mine tells my crew to get down on the floor of the raft, but I am not conscious of making the command. Every synapse in my brain and every muscle in my body is focused on pulling away from that wall. My feet, my thighs, my stomach, my back, my arms, my hands all work together, in a movement that is, I think, very like a wave, to bring the oars upstream against the rushing water. The wall gets closer and closer, and just when I think I am doing no good at all I feel the boat responding, moving backward against the current that's been driving it toward the rock. The nose of the boat barely kisses the wall and one more stroke pulls us safely away.

"Damn," says one of the Texans. "Hot damn."

We go to work rescuing the other boat's passengers.

I am walking down the street in Manhattan, Fifth Avenue in the lower Sixties, women with shopping bags on all sides. I realize with some horror that for the last fifteen blocks I have been counting how many women have better and how many women have worse figures than I do. Did I say fifteen blocks? I meant fifteen years.

I am sitting at my parents' dinner table in the summer between my freshman and sophomore years. I have
brought the first boy I have ever really cared about home
from college, and we are making vaguely interesting small
talk while my mother portions out the food.

I have been at college so long I have forgotten the rules
by which my family eats dinner. I am not allowed to have
bread, dessert, or seconds, ever, and there is an especially
tricky rule that has to do with how much money has been
spent on dinner and whether I am, or am not, supposed to
finish everything that's been put on my plate.

My young boyfriend is telling a story, rather unsuc-
cessfully, that I know to be funny; I'm embarrassed for
him, and I absentmindedly reach for a second helping
of peas.

"You start eating like that," my father barks at me, "and
before too long you'll be as big as a house."

I stare at the spinach coagulating on my plate.

The trick has always been to look only selectively into
the mirror. To see the bright eyes, the shining hair, the
whispered print of the blouse falling open to reveal soft
tanned cleavage, the shapely curve of a taut muscular calf.

My husband manages a restaurant here in town. He employs fifteen twenty-one-year-olds from California. They are all variations on blonde, on tan, on figures drawn to perfection. They call my husband Mick Dundee (after the movie about the human crocodile), which I find particularly revolting; they are the kind of girls who can't talk to a man without touching him. When I come to the restaurant they smile at me politely, curiously, something between wonder and doubt in their eyes. My husband, who is blond and tanned, and also built to perfection, says they do this because I am a published author, but I secretly believe they are trying to imagine what he could possibly see in someone with a body like mine.

My thinnest friend Kris says, "I don't know, but it seems to me that if the only thing that's wrong with you is that you weigh too much, you actually have it pretty good."

"The only thing?" I say to her, calmly. "The only thing?"

I am helicopter skiing in Idaho with a man named John whom I, for no good reason at all, feel the need to impress. Six inches of snow have fallen just after midnight, and under those six inches there's a thick sun-ruined crust. The helicopter leaves us on the dark side of the Tetons. The man I am here with was born in the Sun Valley Lodge; he could ski before he was confidently walking. We are neither lovers nor quite yet friends. We find ourselves on top of this mountain together, practically by accident. And yet I need to ski well in front of him, and that need is almost enough to keep me from being scared.

John hops off the cornice and into the pristine bowl as if he's stepping off a sidewalk, as if it wasn't almost ninety degrees vertical, as if the sun wasn't hitting it and making it tetchy for avalanche, as if there wasn't that crustiness trying to grab his skis from underneath.

My last thought is, *The sooner I go, the less time he'll have to watch me,* so I launch myself, trying to find a rhythm, trying to make figure eights out of his perfect turns. The crust beneath the powder makes a terrible noise as it grips and releases, grips and releases, but I keep turning, thinking about weighting and unweighting my body, thinking about keeping my shoulders in the fall line, thinking about the ever-reliable strength in my knees.

I ski without my normal worst-case scenario tape playing in my head, although here there's more justification for it than usual. I ski way too fast, take too many chances; I become what the ski bums call *focused,* believing entirely in my body's ability to perform correctly, to absorb the slope's imperfections, to ride out the speed. I feel strangely light and incredibly agile, the turns becoming the downbeat in a song it feels like I could play forever. I ski past John, who has stopped to wait for me in a small grove of trees. The tails of my skis send up an arc of powder that coats him, and when I finally stop, ten perfect turns later, his head is thrown back in laughter and he looks like an angel in the snow.

"Hold your tummy in," my mother would yell every morning from the front door as I walked across the lawn to the waiting school bus, as if the bus didn't have open windows, as if what she really meant was goodbye.

My friends Terilynn and thin Kris and I are sitting in a coffee bar talking. I tell them about the girls at Mike's restaurant. Kris tells me I'm crazy, that I have an unrealistic view of my appearance, that those girls would never think such a thing, looking at me. Terilynn, who is imperfectly shaped in several of the same ways I am, is not quite so convinced.

"You're wrong," I tell Kris. "I have a perfectly reasonable idea of my own attractiveness...good legs, shiny eyes, a pretty face, nice hair...On an attractiveness scale of one to a hundred, I'm in the high seventies, and ten pounds thinner, the mid-eighties."

"So what am I?" Kris says.

Both Terilynn and I put her in the high nineties, with a parenthetical reference to the fact that women, coveting her extreme thinness, might put her slightly higher than men.

We give Terilynn a seventy-two, with a high-eighties in-centive if she continues to lose weight.

From there we get a little crazy, rating everyone from Jodie Foster (ninety-one) to Bill Clinton (eighty-four) to Gerard Depardieu (eighty-nine) to Madonna (upon whom we were unable to reconcile, the number ranging from twenty-seven to seventy-eight).

"This is the nineties, girls," the waitress says when she brings us the check. "We're supposed to be into inner beauty now."

Sometimes I'm afraid the main reason I spend half of my life outdoors is simply because there aren't any mirrors.

I'm sitting on my front porch, blank computer screen in front of me, except two words at the top: The body. I am determined to write something positive, having sworn not to spend as much of the second half of my life preoc-cupied with my physical imperfections as I did the first. A woman walks up the street, bone-thin in a running bra, Lycra shorts, and a Walkman. I look down at my shapeless flannel nightgown, my fuzzy slippers, my belly, my hips, and turn my computer off for at least an hour. The woman is striding big confident strides up my street, which is the steepest in our mountain town. She looks as if she will keep that pace right up and over the mountain.

I am hiking to the top of Mount Timpanogos, the highest mountain in my part of Utah, 11,750 feet above sea level, 5,340 above the trailhead where four hours ago I parked my car. Hiking Timpanogos is not scary or life-threatening, it's just grueling, roughly equivalent to starting on the rim of the Grand Canyon and then walking *up* one vertical mile to the river.

The only time safety on Timpanogos becomes an issue is in a sudden summer thunderstorm, when the shale that makes up the last hour of the climb turns slippery and loose, and lightning strikes the part of the mountain that's above the tree line, which for the hiker who gets stranded up there can amount to hours and hours of dodging the heart of the storm.

Today there is only blue sky on my side of the mountain, not so much as a cumulus cloud. Maybe that is why I'm so surprised when I arrive at the summit and see the other half of the sky, horror-film black and crackling with thunder and lightning, sheets of rain like iron curtains walking toward me from a storm center only a few hundred yards away.

The way I see it I have two choices: I can either pick my way between the lightning bolts for a couple of hours and risk a shaley mudslide under combined pressure of the rain and my weight, or I can leap down off the ridge of this mountain and into one of the permanent snowfields that line the mountain's steeper, "unclimbable" side. I won't have to stop exactly, just stay on my feet and do a little boot skiing for maybe ten minutes and a couple of thousand feet down to the bottom of the ice field and tree line. If I lose my footing and start rolling, my problems become a little more complex. I tighten down the straps on my daypack, find the shallowest part of the slope above which to get airborne, and count to three.

On two and a half I realize that no matter how hard I try to find one, there is no scenario of liking my body when it is stationary, no scenario that doesn't take place in a moment of life-or-death athleticism, of do-or-die strength.

I am lying on another table, face up this time, staring at the monkey my gynecologist has pasted to the ceiling to prove he has the sense of humor his schedule doesn't often allow him to show. He is a decent man, direct and gentle, but this is Utah, where men still own women's bodies, so the bills come to my house in some long-since-departed boyfriend's name.

We have our usual birth-control conversation. "What do you get when you cross Dan Quayle with an IUD?" I ask him, and he just shakes his head. I can't help myself. There's something about being in the gynecologist's office that turns me, instantly, into a stand-up comedienne.

This is the big 3-0 visit. A complete physical, my yearly

pelvic, and because I have family history, the first mammo-
gram of my life. The doctor broods over something he
doesn't like in my folder while the nurse makes me get on
the scale. Out of habit, I start apologizing, though the
number turns out to be slightly lower than last year.

"There's something here that troubles me," the doctor
says. "Just wait here a minute while I go call the lab."

"Where's he think I'm gonna go dressed like this?" I
say to the nurse, but my voice cracks apart at the end like a
mirror, my humor shot through with brittle fear. It has
been less than a month since my best friend died of cancer,
less than a year since my mother died of a heart attack, or
long-term starvation, or the sheer displeasure of living
with the things her aging body did.

No diagnosis yet and already the regret is settling in. I
should have loved my body better, should have loved its
curves and folds and softness, should have practiced standing with my pelvis the way Wendy told me to. But instead I
have ignored it, left the cancer to grow in its dark uninhab-
itable recesses; I think of the drawer that holds my summer
T-shirts, where every dark winter the mice move in.

When the nurse leaves the room I pull the hospital
gown to one side and look down at myself, the inch of extra flesh on each hip, the way my belly pushes out in a particularly annoying way that makes the occasional bystander
ask me if I'm pregnant.

A wave of love for my body that is as unfamiliar as it is
terrifying washes over me. I'm afraid at first it is despera-

tion love, the kind I've felt for a man only on the brink of his leaving, but this is more penetrating, all-encompassing; a love so sad and deep and complicated I am left, for a change, without words. I can almost feel the cancer spreading now, one cell at a time through the dark parts of me, and I stand alone in front of the mirror, trying to love it away.

The doctor opens the door and smiles, apologetic. "My mistake," he says, appearing not to notice my nakedness. "You're as healthy as an ox."

"How healthy is an ox?" I say, remembering a *National Geographic* special about oxen getting bugs up their noses that made them go insane, but the doctor is already out the door and with the next patient.

I let my legs go loose and try to stand using only my pelvis. I drop my shoulders as low as they will go and try to think about transferring my body weight (this takes tremendous concentration) to my hips. I take one more long look in the mirror before putting on my clothes.

Fat Lady Nuding

I am fat. I am naked. I am not alone.

This may sound like a nightmare, but I'm awake and reasonably sober, all things considered—this is a "Nude" Year's Eve party and my first nudist experience. I'm here as the guest of a male friend who has been a member of a national nudist organization for a couple of years. He assures me nudism is not about sex, and like everyone else I think, "Yeah, right" but alternately I think, "Thank god," because if nudism were about sex I'd be in the same old situation that I'm in my clothes—a 245-pound body that squashes any hope of fitting into the mainstream mold of sexy at the turn of the twenty-first century. To be honest, at that time in my life, a newly single mother and graduate student after a twenty-year stint as a homemaker and wife, I'd have gone almost anywhere, to almost any length, to find relief from the reminders of my sizable inadequacy.

The party is at a middle-class home in a middle-class suburb in the middle of Ohio. Partygoers range in age from early twenties to mid-sixties. Not everyone is naked. Like me, a few others are first-timers and we are offered a cushion of comfort—"if and when you're ready, get naked." Those who are naked have towels slung over their shoulders, or if sitting, spread under their bottoms. Commandment One of Nudist Etiquette: never nude without your towel; Two, Three, and Four—collapse that erection; don't stare at body parts; no physical familiarity in the nudist "public," even between couples; Five, no photography—with the exception of the permission of close friends; Six and Seven, avoid last names; confidentiality is a must; Eight, Nine, and Ten, never leave home without sunscreen, sunglasses, and sunhat.

I am not exactly the nude life of the party. I'm sitting on the couch, a towel under me, a towel partially over me, or over my belly (sometimes I think she deserves an identity of her own), to hide the blubber that spills onto my upper thighs. My shoulders are naked, and they feel just as I imagined they would feel—at once powerful and vulnerable—when I imagined having a body I could dip and zip into an exquisitely cut off-the-shoulder cocktail dress, a little number in sparkling teal.

Dick Clark is on the television and folks, couples mostly, are piled beside one another on sofas and chairs around the room. The host suggests a game where couples stand face-to-face on telephone books and balance on the balls of their feet while stooping to retrieve a coin from the floor. Those who don't fall off the stack continue to add telephone books to their pile until only one couple is left standing. My friend and I are cajoled to participate, but I am horrified by the idea. I can barely balance Belly when she is tucked tidily into clothing and my feet are firmly planted on the ground.

I enjoy watching this game though. The couples are good sports and make great fun of the experience, tumbling and exaggerating, blaming and laughing. I almost forget they are nude, until I realize the last couples standing are slender and sculpted, lithe and coordinated, and I am suddenly aware of the weight of myself, the sweat collecting in the skin-to-skin connection between my belly and my thighs. I shift Belly around self-consciously beneath the towel. As I admire these bodies, as I study their definition and agility, their symmetry and mobility, I am awed. I am jealous and resentful. I am frustrated and angry. Since puberty I've worked at manipulating my body. The harder I worked to be skinny the faster I grew fatter. The deeper my longing to be beautiful the more ugly the reflection in the mirror.

I am fat. I am naked. I am alone.

Years before this Nude Year's Eve Party, when I am a housewife from Cleveland, a mother of three sons, which I bore in four years' time, I am home alone. My sons are at school, my husband at work. I transport this body and me, weighing around 264 pounds, into the shower. The spray pulsates rhythmically and I wish the hot water was endowed with the magic to wash me away. I am again on some diet that isn't working—that *I'm* not working, because isn't fat, after all, the fault of the fatty who wears it? Isn't the fat caused by some flaw in Fatty's character? Some lack of willpower? Or a lack of exercise? A lack of work ethic or lack of self-respect? Isn't the fat the fault of some aspect of Fatty's behavior that is out of control? Wouldn't Fatty be thin—wouldn't I be thin—if I wasn't seriously flawed? If I wasn't a bad person? A weak person? A needy person? Wouldn't I be thin if I just didn't cry so easily? If I didn't want so much of my husband's attention? If I didn't need so much respite from the demands of my three young sons? Wouldn't I be thin if I only had more energy? More motivation? More brains? Wouldn't I be thin if I could only fully grasp the dire consequences of living fat?

So I let the hot, hotter, hottest water punish me, scald me. Last night I once again paid my $15 to the diet club and gained instead of lost. Nine weeks of weighing and measuring food, of weighing and measuring me, and only seven pounds of liberation to show for my effort. At 264 pounds, I weigh too much to lose at this rate. Other

women my size drop seven pounds the first week. But I
cheat. Don't I? But I didn't cheat the first week. But I don't
measure and weigh every morsel that passes over my lips. I
don't keep a tedious account of my food intake in my food
diary. I don't keep my exercise log. In fact, I don't exercise
enough; I have never exercised enough. I fear I can never
ever exercise enough to escape the fat. Or if I could, all I
could do is exercise and nothing else. I would wake up and
start moving, jumping, twisting, walking, skipping, running, dancing, jogging. From morning to evening I would
move, shake this body, and the fat would cling to me, claw
at me, laugh in my face.

I cry now: furtive tears sneaking through the shower
spray; drip-drop tears, drip down one side; drop down the
other, little pulses of pain escaping my optimism. About
now, I usually talk to myself. I am a great talker to myself, a
veritable jukebox of what-doesn't-kill-you-will-make-you-
stronger speeches. But I am broken today. The inner coach
is silent. The fat lady is screaming.

"Shut up in there," I yell back. "Shut up!"

I hit myself: fist against sternum. I heave. Sob. Beat my
belly. Pummel it. I hate this body. I hate it. I am not a fat
person. I am not. I am smart and funny and pretty and lik-
able. I am competent and hardworking. This body, this fat
bitch of a body, betrays me. Lies about me. I hate it. Like I
hate these diets. Like I hate little frozen boxed desserts and
perfectly rounded half cups of rice. Like I hate tuna fish,
like I hate all kinds of fish. Like I hate scales and plus sizes

and protein exchanges and exercise journals. Like I hate this body.

Without mercy, I beat. I am my own punching bag. I beat because I am fat. I beat because I won't quit: I won't quit eating; I won't quit dieting. I beat because I won't own my fat. I beat because I won't stop fighting my fat. I beat because I lie to myself and weigh myself and do what all good American girls should do: try to lose weight. I beat because each week I line up to go behind the partitioned wall where the scale has been given a throne of its own. I beat because I remove every extraneous article of clothing and all accessories and submit myself to the doctor's scale, to the mechanical contraption that has been given the power to determine the quality of the relationship I have with my body.

I beat because I repeatedly stand on a paper towel on the wobbly platform and let the clerk toggle a weight back and forth so she can account for every last ounce. I beat because she will write my loss or gain on a white card that acts as my self-esteem passport into the next week: If the number diminished, I can feel optimistic about my awful self; if it increased, I can deal myself the appropriate punishment. Not always this physical beating. The berating of my conscience is more than enough. And whether I lost two pounds (eight sticks of margarine!) or gained half a pound, I will hate me more for submitting myself to this size-four-size-six-size-eight-branding of the female body. I will use this hate, this anger, to pretend that after the weigh-in and before the next morning, I am in a free zone—free calories, free carbs—and I will sit through the meeting led by a woman who prides herself in not having eaten a candy bar in over four years and nod at her approvingly and consider which restaurant I will steal into before I haul my fat body back home to my husband and my children. I will contemplate whether I will eat pizza or fried chicken, whether I will have mashed potatoes with gravy or a milk shake or both. Once I am stuffed past the point of any pleasure, I walk through the kitchen door and see last week's food diary on the fridge. "I will do better this week," I will say, knowingly making a false promise to myself, an act I would never tolerate toward another person. But I am not just any person. I am fat and flawed. I am undeserving and unforgivable.

I am fat. I am naked. I am not alone.

I am now up and moving about naked at the Nude Year's party. I find I am not so self-conscious about Belly while standing up. She still sinks to the top of my thighs like a pair of bottom boobies, but at least she is not folded and bunched up in my lap. The fact is I'm not very self-conscious at all. I want to account for this—to explain why and how my belly and me could be bare naked in a room

full of other bare-naked bodies without feeling compelled
to cover up, but I feel no such compulsion. In fact, the
skin-to-air connection is soothing and the bareness feels
freeing.

At midnight, some of the crazier among us, including
me (how quickly I fall), dip daringly into the subzero wind
chills to holler "Happy Nude Year." Two naked men make
snow angels. Both return indoors squealing like scalded
pigs. In fact, we're all cold enough to justify adorning our
nude selves with the festive accessories we were encouraged to bring as part of our Nude Year's "costume." I just
happened to bring along my boas. With a spin in the magi-
cian's closet and the whoosh of a few colorful feathers,
Delilah and Boas replace Donna and Belly. The feathers
are received with such admiration, for a moment I forget
my fat and give the pink and black swags around my neck
and waist a few swanky swirls. When the group claps, I
laugh and add some hip action.

Someone, I can't remember who, brings out body
paint, and there I am, at 1:30 on January 1, letting my
friend paint a yellow and black abstract over my belly and
breasts. The paint is cold and the brush tickles, and I think
his work is quite a bit short of showing any signs of genius, but I am enjoying this, enjoying having someone paint
Belly while I'm naked in normal lighting and surrounded
by a roomful of strangers. While others pose to have animal likenesses painted on various body parts, I notice that

no one seems the least bit self-conscious. No one is embarrassed or ashamed. And no one is staring at me in disbelief at my disproportion.

As our final activity before breakfast and heading home, partygoers volunteer to get letters painted on their bottoms and then line up, butts thrust toward the camera, to display the evening's blessing, HAPPY NUDE YEAR. I am not ready to participate in such a display, but I do take some pleasure in painting letters on the bottom of others' butts. Each butt has its own personality. Some wiggle flamboyantly in front of the brush; others are a little shy and want me to hurry. These rear ends I paint come in various shapes and sizes, but I can recognize each one as belonging to another human being.

The flash of the camera signals breakfast. As we head toward the kitchen to fill our plates, someone I don't know catches my arm. "Turn around here," he says. "Let me see your masterpiece."

The Nude Year's Eve party is winding down. As we eat an early morning breakfast at the dining room table, I don't say much—I have a lot to digest, so to speak—but I listen to people talk of what they do when they aren't nuding. Vocations and hobbies vary as much as butt size, but what I notice most is that I find these individuals interesting and thoughtful and diverse. I am among anthropologists and artists and farmers and engineers, information technologists and inventory controllers. We are overproportioned and underproportioned, unremarkably so. Scarred and blemished, our bodies are hewn to tell our stories. We are living art that bears the marks of individual craftsmanship.

I can't say I don't sense any discomfort about my body size in others—one woman, a tiny woman who takes up a great big space with her Pamela A–like proportions— avoids looking at me. While others smile and introduce themselves, I feel as if I am invisible to her. Belly, I imagine, is simply more than she bargained for at a nudist event. For god's sake, no one of my unbearable proportions would have the nerve to bare all. I am too much of an in-your-face reminder of what can happen if she succumbs to her appetite or neglects her aerobics. Despite her inability to accommodate me, I can't find among this group of nudists the judgment or the pity or the hostility or the distaste that I can experience when I'm fully and tastefully dressed in my size twenty-four clothes strolling through the shopping mall.

I am fat. I am naked. I am not alone.

I feel the essence of a New Year around this table. I feel hope, hope that I'm not as repulsive as I've believed. Hope that I can rest for a while; rest from the weighing and the measuring of myself and food—rest from these practices that have become little more than acts of self-hate. I feel hope that maybe I can play from inside this body;

move around from inside here; have fun from in here. That maybe I could love and make love from in here.

I feel hope that I could live in this bulky body as is, no size contingencies attached, a hope that maybe I'm more than the big fat sum of my weight, that I am simply, but sizably, human.

Permissions Acknowledgments

Contributors

SARAH FENSKE originally wrote "Big Game Hunters" for *Scene,* the alt weekly in Cleveland where she worked for two years. A Cleveland native, she's won awards for her investigative, environmental, and medical coverage. She currently lives in Houston, Texas, and writes about politics and crime for the *Houston Press.*

ATUL GAWANDE is a surgeon and frequent contributor to many magazines, including *Salon* and the *New Yorker.* His book, *Complications: A Surgeon's Notes on an Imperfect Science,* was nominated for the 2002 National Book Award.

LORI GOTTLIEB, a commentator for National Public Radio, is author of the national bestseller, *Stick Figure: A Diary of My Former Self,* an American Library Association "Best Books 2001" selection and a Borders "Original New Voice" title. Most recently, she was a staff writer on the new NBC/Bravo series *Significant Others,* a sitcom about marital dysfunction.

PAM HOUSTON is the author of two collections of linked short stories, *Cowboys Are My Weakness* and *Waltzing the Cat,* and a collection of autobiographical essays, *A Little More About Me.* Houston also edited *Women on Hunting: Essays, Fiction, and Poetry,* and wrote the text for *Men Before Ten A.M.,* a book of photographs by the French photographer Véronique Vial. Currently, she is an associate professor in the writing program at University of California, Davis.

NATALIE KUSZ is the author of the memoir, *Road Song.* Her short nonfiction, poetry, and book reviews have appeared in numerous journals and anthologies, including *Harper's, McCall's, The Threepenny Review, Utne Reader, New York Times,* and *Best American Essays.* Her work has earned a Whiting Writer's Award and a Pushcart Prize, and she's been awarded fellowships from Radcliffe College's Bunting Institute and the National Endowment for the Arts. She teaches creative writing at Eastern Washington University.

STEPHEN KUUSISTO is the author of *Planet of the Blind: A Memoir* and *Only Bread, Only Light,* and editor of *The Poet's Notebook: Excerpts from the Notebooks of Contemporary American Poets.* He is a frequent commentator on National Public Radio and lectures widely on disability and public policy.

ANNE LAMOTT is the author of six novels, including *Hard Laughter, Rosie, Joe Jones, All New People, Blue Shoe,* and *Crooked Little Heart.* In addition, she has authored three bestselling works of nonfiction: *Operating Instructions,* an account of life as a single mother during her son's first year; *Bird by Bird: Some Instructions on Writing and Life,* a guide to writing and the challenges of a writer's life; and *Traveling Mercies,* a collection of autobiographical essays on faith.

VICTOR LAVALLE is the author of *Slapboxing with Jesus* and *The Ecstatic,* which was a finalist for the PEN/Faulkner Award in 2002 and winner of the Hurston/Wright Legacy Award in 2003.

MICHAEL MARTONE is the author of several fiction and nonfiction collections, including *The Blue Guide to Indiana, Seeing Eye, Pensées: The Thoughts of Dan Quayle, Fort Wayne Is Seventh on Hitler's List,* and *The Flatness and Other Landscapes,* a collection of essays about the Midwest that received the 1998 AWP Award for Creative Nonfiction. He teaches creative writing at the University of Alabama, Tuscaloosa.

CHERYL PECK lives with her cat, Babycakes, in Three Rivers, Michigan. She is the author of *Fat Girls and Lawn Chairs.*

DAVID SEDARIS is the author of the bestsellers *Barrel Fever* and *Holidays on Ice,* as well as collections of personal essays, *Naked, Me Talk Pretty One Day,* and *Dress Your Family in Corduroy and Denim.* His essays appear regularly in *Esquire* and the *New Yorker.*

STEVEN A. SHAW is the publisher of fat-guy.com and co-founder and executive director of the eGullet Society for Culinary Arts & Letters. He is a food writer and lawyer and the winner of the 2002 James Beard Foundation Journalism Award for Internet Writing. He was a frequent contributor to *Salon.*

Attorney SONDRA SOLOVAY is the author of *Tipping the Scales of Justice: Fighting Weight-Based Discrimination.* She has received three awards from the National Association to Advance Fat Acceptance (NAAFA): in 1998 for her work on the defense team in *California v. Corrigan,* in 1999 for her work with the San

Francisco Human Rights Commission, and in 2000 for helping amend San Francisco's antidiscrimination ordinance to include height and weight.

SALLIE TISDALE is the author of *The Sorcerer's Apprentice, Harvest Moon, Lot's Wife, Stepping Westward, Talk Dirty to Me,* and *The Best Thing I Ever Tasted: The Secret of Food.* She was a columnist for *Salon,* and is a contributing editor at *Harper's.*

IRVIN D. YALOM, M.D., is professor emeritus of psychiatry at Stanford University. He continues his clinical practice and lectures widely in the United States. His training tapes are frequently used in programs for therapists. Dr. Yalom lives in Palo Alto, California.